P9-DVL-991

# MEDIA MAZE

## UNCONVENTIONAL WISDOM FOR GUIDING CHILDREN THROUGH MEDIA

# ERIC RASMUSSEN, PHD

PLAIN SIGHT PUBLISHING
AN IMPRINT OF CEDAR FORT, INC.
SPRINGVILLE, UTAH

For my wife and daughters, who are each extraordinary

ISBN 13: 978-1-4621-2122-9

Published by Plain Sight Publishing, an imprint of Cedar Fort, Inc., 2373 W. 700 S., Springville, UT 84663
Distributed by Cedar Fort, Inc. www.cedarfort.com

Library of Congress Control Number: 2017948147

Cover design by Priscilla Chaves
Back cover design by M. Shaun McMurdie
Cover design © 2017 by Cedar Fort, Inc.
Edited and typeset by Erica Myers

Printed in the United States of America

10  9  8  7  6  5  4  3  2  1

Printed on acid-free paper

# Praise for *Media Maze: Unconventional Wisdom for Guiding Children through Media*

As a scholar, a preeminent researcher, and a father to media-savvy kids, Eric Rasmussen not only asks the right questions but works to prove his theories on how media affects kids. His book is an expertly crafted guide to some of the most vexing problems faced by parents today. Through inspiring personal stories and clear insight into the science behind media, his *Media Maze* gives solutions to parents struggling with the onslaught of screens. In the same way he shed light on how *Daniel Tiger's Neighborhood* positively impacts kids, after reading *Media Maze*, parents will have more of those "aha!" moments and will no longer look at media, or their own kids, the same way again.

—Angela Santomero, creator of *Daniel Tiger's Neighborhood* and *Blue's Clues*, and founding partner & chief creative officer of Out of the Blue Enterprises

*Media Maze* takes a refreshing, and very much needed, approach to helping families address the complex and daunting world of kids and media. It empowers parents, respects children, and considers the very real context of a technology pervasive world. As a parent, it gave me well-researched, practical ideas for how to better engage my own children around media. As a fellow scholar, it gave me hope that our hard-fought research in this space has found a great outlet for impact.

—Alison Bryant, PhD, president and founder of PlayScience

Kids today are immersed in media like fish in water. Some media can be harmful too, like contaminated water. Parents need help navigating their kids through today's media-saturated world. Dr. Eric Rasmussen's book can be a great help in this regard. It is important to point out that the advice Dr. Rasmussen gives in this book is not based on his own opinion. Rather, it is based on research evidence from scientific studies. Just as important, Dr. Rasmussen makes the research evidence accessible to ordinary readers. Moreover, the writing style is engaging and interesting. I highly recommend this book to all parents who are concerned about the media their children are consuming.

—Brad J. Bushman, PhD, professor of communication and psychology, The Ohio State University

# CONTENTS

# 1 The Lost Generation

I don't know anybody more full of life than our teenage daughter. When she's happy, the world is a beautiful place. Her moods seem to radiate and extend to everyone around her. She kisses the top of my head and tells me good night, every night. As the old cliché goes, she wears her emotions on her sleeve. The good and bad ones. When she's mad, she slams doors and screams. She seems to never have anything to wear, and of course it's usually my fault. She's sometimes scatterbrained. She loves being around people. She likes to eat out, and she especially loves when her best friend's mom brings her fast food for lunch at school. She befriends lonely classmates. She could do better in math class. She likes setting goals, but hates following through on them. She loves Disney music. She loves Taylor Swift, though like many teenage girls, she might refuse to admit it. And she leaves her cell phone on the couch, right where I usually sit. Every. Single. Day.

Ah, her cell phone. She bought her first phone when she turned thirteen, and she used it in the exact way you would expect a middle school girl would use a smart phone. She was the stereotypical, teen tech junkie. To her credit, she saved up and bought the phone herself and pays her own monthly phone bill. But our world turned upside down the day it came through our front door. No more than two hours after we activated her phone, she had received a collect call from an inmate at the local prison, carried on a text conversation with a stranger, and left a voicemail for her grandmother while on a phone call with a friend.

Talk about jumping right into the media parenting fire. I'm sure similar scenarios have played out in homes all across America. Teenager gets phone. Teenager learns how to text. Teenager discovers emojis. Teenager feels naked without her phone in hand. Teenager talks to you without looking up from the phone in her hands. Indeed, media technologies have changed our world. And they're still changing our world.

Although we've resolved many of the issues we faced after she first got her phone, our daughter is still pretty attached to it. She always has to have music on, even while doing homework. It's hard to carry on a text conversation with her because of all the emojis—I simply don't know what they all mean. Especially the one that looks like either a swirl of soft-serve chocolate ice cream or a pile of poop. Which is it? If she can't spend time on the tablet playing games, watching YouTube videos, or catching the latest episode of her favorite sketch comedy, she becomes a restless ball of complaining energy. Sometimes, it's all we can do as parents to convince her to do something besides look at a screen.

At this point, you might be expecting me, someone with a doctorate who studies children and media for a living, to sound the call for parents to wait as long as they can before they let their kids have a phone. In fact, many "experts" on social media do just this—they share a story about a really bad experience their child had with a smart phone and conclude that every child should be banned from ever owning such a device. You might expect me to similarly lament how phones, the Internet, and social media have become the "digital heroin"[1] from which kids can't escape. Conventional wisdom would suggest that someone like me would be a little more vigilant than the average person when it comes to media parenting. Conventional wisdom would suggest that it's my job to participate in the scaremongering we see on social media. And conventional wisdom would suggest that someone like me would say we should do all we can to protect our children's innocence by shielding them from media for as long as we can.

But the more I research, the more I'm convinced that the time for conventional wisdom is past. As the title of this book states, it's time for some unconventional wisdom.

## Unconventional Wisdom

I'm just going to drop the bombshell now in as clear language as I can. When it comes to children and media, I'm not worried about children. When it comes to media, I'm concerned about parents.

A simple history lesson will help illustrate why I've come to this conclusion. For many of us, we grew up without the Internet. The media we had as children consisted of TV, radio, newspapers, magazines, and that old set of encyclopedias on the living room shelf. When I was in high school, my dad told me about an idea he had for an invention. He wanted to create something that he called a Scorebox. One thing that really bugged my dad was being unable to keep up with his favorite sports teams while he was out and about at his daughters' dance recitals or his sons' sports games. Back then, we actually had to watch TV or listen to the radio to get updates on game scores. Seems so inconvenient now, doesn't it? I remember my dad telling me that the technology was being developed that would allow you to see scores from any sports game at any time if you had a Scorebox that could connect to satellites. At the time, it sounded so far-fetched to me. The stuff of science fiction. Now, of course, it's commonplace. It's called the Internet.

Fast-forward twenty years. The current generation of parents is the first generation in the history of the world that has had to parent in a world that is completely immersed in media. Every way we turn, we see media. It's in our children's faces. It's in their pockets. It's such a part of life now that it's hard to imagine life without media. Not too long ago, our Wi-Fi at home turned off for about five minutes, and from all the grumbling I heard, you would have thought someone had dumped a pile of manure in our living room. Parents today can't ask their parents how they approached media parenting, because their parents never lived through what we're living through. It's like we've been placed inside a giant maze without a map and have been told to get our children out before the boogie monster catches them. Even if we had a map, the media maze changes every day as new social media platforms and technologies are developed. We don't know what's around the next corner.

So, yes, I'm concerned about parents. I'm concerned about our ability to guide kids through a maze that we know nothing about. When I see kids glued to their phones, I don't blame the kids. How can we blame them for doing what all their peers are doing? No, when I think of the effect of media exposure on children, my thoughts inevitably turn to the state of media parenting. Is it parents' fault that we don't know how to deal with media? Maybe. Is it a function of the rapid pace of technological advancement? Maybe. It's probably a mixture of a host of things, but any way I look at media parenting, it's clear that parents need some sort of map, some sort of guide, to help them help their children. And I'm not talking about another social media pundit or self-proclaimed parenting expert offering advice. What parents need is to be armed with strategies that are based on decades of research on the media's effect on children.

I feel so strongly about this because research shows that parents are the single most powerful influence in a child's life when it comes to almost anything, including media. There is no one in a better position to change how kids are affected by the media than a parent. There is no one that has more influence, who cares more, and who knows their own child better than a parent. The problem doesn't start with how much children use the media and all the yucky, no-good stuff that comes with it. The problem starts with parents. American parents, by and large, do not know what media parenting means. When it comes to the media, today's parents are media illiterate to a severe degree. I'm not necessarily blaming parents—we've been thrown into this digital world just as our kids have been. So, I'm not convinced we've lost a generation of children to the media. What we're losing is a generation of parents. Parents today have either forgotten, simply don't know, or have a mutated concept of what it means to parent when it comes to media.

Now, before you go feeling guilty on me, the very fact that you're reading this right now means that you're already different than most parents. You already know that you have an influence. So, for you, this book is not meant to make you feel guilty, but to help you realize how powerful you really are.

I learned the power of media parenting from my own parents. I live more than 1,500 miles from my parents. I get to see them about once a year when they come to visit. One night during one of their recent stays at our house, we got to talking about my childhood and some of the things I did that they didn't know about. For example, one time when I was twelve, a friend and I arranged to meet some girls at the movie theater under the pretext of a guys' night out. I don't remember the movie, but I remember holding a girl's hand during it. There were also other things I did, of course. There are things you did that your parents didn't know about—the typical teenager stuff that we all did. But I had another media-related experience that neither my wife nor my parents had ever heard of until this recent chat with my parents.

Remember that I grew up in the '90s, and as I've already mentioned, the Internet was not yet a thing. So, while it was still possible, it was a little harder for a boy to get his hands on erotic pictures of women. But if you wanted to find it, you could. In high school I played sports, and before each home game, we would go to the house of one of the guys on the team and have dinner. One night, the parents left the house where we were having our team dinner. One minute they were there, and the next they were gone. So, there we were, a bunch of adolescent guys with nothing to do but eat. Any guesses as to what a group of adolescent guys does when there are no parents around? From seemingly out of nowhere, a VHS tape appeared and was inserted into the VCR. I had a good hunch what was on the video, and I was pretty sure it wasn't a Bible documentary or an episode of *Care Bears*. I had three choices. First, I could watch the video with my teammates, and a part of me wanted to. If there ever was a time in my life when I felt peer pressure to do something that I had been taught not to do, this was it. Second, I could leave the dinner. But this option was no good, because after the team dinner, I had to drive some of the guys to the school for our game. And last, I could go into another room by myself while my teammates did whatever it is boys do when they watch porn. It must have been my parents who taught me about the negative consequences of viewing pornography. They must have hammered it home pretty good, because at that moment of decision, their words came back to my mind. Their words collided with the adolescent curiosity I felt. My parents' words won out that day. I decided to stay in the kitchen and eat by myself until it was time to go to the school for the game. In that moment, I felt very alone. I got teased and ribbed about it by my teammates. I don't fault them for watching the video. I think most teenage guys would. For them, it wasn't wrong—they likely hadn't had the same lessons I'd had about pornography since it wasn't so prolific back then. What rule were they breaking? But for me, it was wrong because I had been taught in a very clear way that looking at pornography was not something my parents wanted me to do. For me, it would have been breaking a rule. So, even though I felt alone, even though my reputation as one of the guys took a hit, and even though I wouldn't quite fit in as one of the guys for the rest of my high school years, I could live with myself and be in the presence of my parents without feeling that I had traded the values they taught me for a few tantalizing moments.

Talking to kids works.

Today's crazy world is very different than the world of our own childhood. Just as today's generation of parents is the first that has had to deal with this media maze, the current generation of kids is the first generation in the history of the world that spends more time looking at a screen than they do sleeping.[2] In his book *Media Literacy*, communication scholar W. James Potter shared some statistics about the digital world in which we are raising our children:

- YouTube is growing at a rate of 100 hours of new video every minute.
- Publishers release 1,500 new books every day.
- Radio stations broadcast nearly 70 million hours of content each year.
- The Internet is composed of about 70 billion webpages.
- There are more than 2 billion Internet users on the planet.
- Together, these Internet users compose and send about 300 billion e-mails, 500 million tweets, and upload about 100 million photos to Facebook *every day.*[3]

Our children have unprecedented access to information. So much good comes from access to all this information. At the same time, however, our brains—and especially children's brains—can't keep up. It's like we're standing underneath Niagara Falls, trying to catch a certain drop of water, but we don't know which drop it is that we're supposed to catch. Today, kids are bombarded with media messages telling them what it means to be a girl or boy, what clothes they should wear, what food they should eat, what words they should use, what morals and values are important and which aren't (or whether morals even exist), what they are supposed to look like, what car they should drive, what beer they should drink, when to have sex, when to rebel against authority, how big certain body parts should be, what color their hair should be, how to treat each other, what country it's okay to bomb, when violence is justified, and the list goes on.

In our media parenting efforts, parents today cannot rely on the experiences we had with media when we were growing up. They are not the same experiences our children are having. When I say today's generation of parents is media illiterate, I mean it. We have no idea what it's like to be a child or a teenager today. We can't truly have sympathy for the media situation in which our children find themselves because we haven't lived what they are living. So how are we supposed to do this? How do we help our kids navigate the media maze in which they live? How do we protect them? Better yet, how do we turn the sympathy we do feel for our children into media parenting strategies capable of protecting our kids?

I'd like to offer some answers to these questions. In fact, the whole reason I wrote this book is because the time I've spent in research related to children and media has made the answers pretty clear. But be aware that the answers to these questions might throw you for a loop. The answers will likely turn your approach to media parenting on its head. While countless parenting books and "expert" advice articles focus on *protecting* our kids from media content, this book provides research-based evidence that our media parenting should focus on *empowering* kids to deal with media content. I'm suggesting that we *stop* trying so hard to protect and shield our kids from all the stuff in the media we don't want them to see, and *start* giving them the tools to deal with what they'll inevitably see in the media.

On the surface, it might seem like there's a big problem with this change in approach to media parenting. When parents (including me) think of media, the protective parenting instinct lights up in us. My wife calls this the mama-bear instinct. "Nothing messes with our children," we say to ourselves. So we do everything in our power to protect our kids. For example, when our oldest daughter was a toddler, we once caught an early morning flight to go visit family over the holidays. Anybody who's ever had a toddler knows that a tired toddler is a whiny toddler. And sure enough, our toddler whined the entire cross-country trip. Sympathetic parents offered us crayons, stuffed animals, books, and toys. That day, however, nothing kept our daughter quiet. She whined the entire four-hour flight, disrupting the early morning sleep of the passengers around us. We were *that* family on the plane. Near the end of the flight, the man sitting in front of us finally had enough. He turned around, looked our toddler in the eye, and asked, "Can't you do anything besides cry?" I felt, more than saw, the mama bear raging through the veins of my wife's neck. Before she did something she would regret, like tear the man's eyes out, I reached my arms around her and held her back. We didn't need to deal with a whiny toddler and air marshals subduing a raging mother. The instinct to protect is real.

I, too, have experienced the protective parenting instinct. Our toddler grew up, as kids do, and became a dancer. A ballerina. It's on the dance floor that she feels most at home. When she reached the "apprentice" level at her dance company, she was required to start partnering with boys. After I got over the fact that a boy's hands would be on my daughter's waist, I learned that they were practicing lifts. When I think of a boy lifting a girl into the air I always think of my wife. She was a cheerleader in college and was once dropped on her back by her cheer partner. She still suffers occasional back pain from that injury (pain that can sometimes predict the weather, by the way), and that was with a cheer partner who had pretty big biceps. Now, a skinny-armed teenage kid was going to lift my daughter into the air. So, naturally, my first thought was, *Kid, if you drop my daughter, I will hunt you down and make you wish you had never been born.*

Wanting to protect and defend our kids is natural, instinctual, and normal. Is protecting our kids bad? Of course not. In fact, I think it's good. But what I'm proposing, and what we'll learn in this book, is that research shows that there is something better than protecting our kids.

## Protecting Our Kids Is Good, but *Empowering* Our Kids Is Great

To put this unconventional media parenting approach into perspective, it might help to understand a few things about me. First and foremost, I am a husband and father. I became a father in the summer of 2001. I was twenty-two years old, and I was scared out of my mind. On the day we took our newborn daughter home from the hospital, I experienced what I'm sure many new parents experience. A wave of panic overtook me as we left the hospital that day. I could not fathom why anybody would let me take this child home. Didn't they know that I knew nothing about kids, let alone a newborn baby? But as parents do, we brought our baby home, we survived the first few sleepless months, and we got into a routine. We began to settle in as a little family, and the fear I felt on the day she was born slowly subsided. We were all sleeping a little better at night, both literally and figuratively. And then September 11th crumpled my secure little world.

Like many people, when I saw the towers come down that day, I left work and went home to be with my family. As I looked at my baby girl, I was once again struck with terror at how ill prepared I was to raise a child in a world where horrible things like that could happen. I felt powerless to protect her. This was not the world I envisioned for my daughter. I wanted a safe world. A peaceful world. One filled with playdates and butterflies, picnics and tea parties. There was no room in my vision of her future for bad things to happen. I'm confident most parents felt this way.

Life, of course, was never the same for us or for anybody else after September 11th, but life demanded that we seek again for normalcy. And because kids don't stop growing, we again settled into a routine. Months passed and our daughter grew. She was healthy and strong. A firecracker like her mom, just as I hoped she'd be. We were living in Utah at the time, plodding our way through my bachelor's degree. Then, one night on the news we learned that Elizabeth Smart had been kidnapped right out of her Salt Lake City bedroom. Immediately, I went and checked to ensure that all the windows in our apartment were locked. This wasn't some tragedy in a distant city. This was just down the road. My fear from September 11th was still somewhat fresh, and now this? Is our world really a place where kids aren't safe even in their own homes? How could I protect my kids from bad things happening to them? Again, I felt totally ill prepared.

All these years later, I still have many of those feelings of inadequacy. I hate the thought that some things in this world are out of my control. It is hard to accept that I can't protect my kids from everything. I know I am not alone in feeling this way. This is why we hear about "helicopter parents" and about parents who "bubble wrap" their kids. This is why we hear news reports about people calling the cops on parents for letting their kids play outside alone, in their own fenced-in backyard. Parents are paranoid about kids' safety, and perhaps rightfully so. I think we feel like if we are extra vigilant that we can keep bad things from happening to our kids. We convince ourselves that bad things don't happen to kids of good parents. We come to believe that we can control life.

But I've learned that we are deceiving ourselves if we think we can control life. The truth is, although we can control our own actions, we cannot control the actions of others. Bad things are going to happen in the world, even to good people. Bad things will happen to our kids. Their feelings will get hurt. Their hearts will be broken. They will get sick. Some will suffer from painful and debilitating illnesses. Some will struggle in school. Some will deal with learning disabilities. Others will suffer from mental illness or addiction. The list of things that could possibly harm our children is endless. The list of things that are beyond our control goes on and on. No wonder we want to circle the wagons and protect with all our might. It's instinctual. It's a parent's job, right?

But even with all the bad stuff going on in society, most of our kids will grow up with what we might call a normal childhood. They'll get up each morning and go to school. They'll participate in sports. They'll have a roof over their head and will have enough to eat. We'll still be vigilant about their physical safety. But as my children have grown, I have found that I worry less about the physical harm that could happen to them than I do about things in life that could alter who they become as a person. I want more than anything for my kids to grow up to be good people. I want them to have a sense of self-worth. I want them to have a desire to help others, to serve in their communities, to have a desire to make the world a better place. I want them to be the person that helps those who are bullied. I want to hear their teachers tell me what great kids I have. And when I think about the people I hope they will *become*, I inevitably think about all the things that could influence that process of becoming. Perhaps one of the most important and powerful of those influences is the media. Today, research shows that kids spend a majority of their waking hours looking at a screen. To me, this means that I should spend less time worrying about my kids getting kidnapped or plane crashes or mass shootings. Instead, I should spend more of my efforts being involved with my kids' media-related experiences, but not in the way we've been doing it. Because our kids live in an unconventional world, our media parenting must also be unconventional.

This book is about coming to terms with the fact that we can't protect our kids from everything in the media. We can set rules about our kids' media use. We can prevent them from getting a smart phone. We can ban video games, movies, and social media. But regardless of how protective and conscientious our media parenting is, our kids will still be exposed to media messages with which we are uncomfortable. I'll go even further by suggesting that not only will our kids be exposed to media messages that make us uncomfortable, but they will see things that make us want to throw up, that make us want to wrap them up in pillows and put them in a padded room for the rest of their lives. And there is no protection that we as parents can provide that will keep our children from seeing these things.

But we can *empower* our kids with the tools to deal with those messages when they come. And they will come. I can't remember where I first heard the following phrase, but some form of it has been attributed to

Martin Luther: "You can't stop a bird from landing on your head; but you *can* stop him from building a nest."[4] In other words, our job isn't to protect our kids from the media birds that might land on their head, it's to keep the media birds from building a nest. Those are two very different things.

## Research-Based Unconventional Wisdom

So let's introduce the academic world in which I live. Daily, I am immersed in research related to the media's effect on children. I design studies, meet with families, write reports about what we find, and then publish the findings in academic journals. I love my job. I'm one of the lucky ones that has found what I feel is my calling in life. But there is one thing that really bothers me about my job. I spend months, sometimes years, working on a research project. I then write it up and send the research paper to an academic journal, where it may or may not get published. But guess how many people read articles published in academic journals? About seven. The Facebook posts of my kids' back-to-school photos receive more likes than there are people who read my journal articles. That is one of the biggest travesties and challenges for us in the field of children and media. Rarely does our research get into the hands of the people who need it most—parents! What good is our research if it sits on a digital shelf where only people with specific academic credentials can access it?

For example, my doctoral dissertation looked at the role of parent-child conversations in minimizing the effects of watching violent cartoons on children's aggression. I was, and still am, extremely proud of that research project. The day my dissertation was bound into an official book nearly two hundred pages long and placed on the shelves of the library at The Ohio State University will remain one of the greatest days of my life. That day, I brought a copy of my dissertation home and asked my wife to read it. I had no doubt that my work of the past four years would change her life in an instant. She opened it up, but after about three minutes, she handed it back to me and said that none of it made any sense. I learned a painful lesson: for someone who doesn't do exactly what I do, reading academic research is like reading the instruction manual for a piece of IKEA furniture in Swedish. That's great, if you speak Swedish. There is much in the field of media research that even I have a hard time understanding, and I read this stuff every day. This is a problem. This is a *big* problem.

So let's map out what we'll do in this book. You want strategies. Strategies that are practical, that are written in the language of the everyday parent, that you can start implementing today. The second half of this book is all about those strategies. The first few chapters set the stage for those strategies. Chapter 2 will increase your awareness of what kids are viewing in the media by going into detail about how much children are exposed to several different types of media content, including what kids encounter online. We'll then spend Chapter 3 discussing how children are affected by media content. Using research and pop culture examples, we'll dig deep into how kids are affected by the various types of media that they see. And because it is not enough to know that kids *are* affected by media, we'll delve into the minds of children and share the science behind *why* kids are influenced by media content in Chapter 4. After setting the stage in this way, Chapters 5–8 present practical, unconventional strategies that parents can start using today in order to help empower kids in a way that will help them navigate the media maze. If you want to jump straight to the strategies, please do. But the strategies will make much more sense with the background provided in the first half of the book. Finally, in the last chapter, we'll get a glimpse into what I think is the future of media research, including concepts related to children's developing brains and how their freedom of thought is intertwined with everything else we discuss in this book.

In each chapter, we'll translate the science behind research on children and media into language meant for parents. You'll encounter some things that make you squirm, especially in the first half of the book. But keep in mind that this is not a doomsday book about the media and how evil it is and how it will corrupt the values and morals of America's children. Nor is it my desire to scare you into banning television, throwing out the smart phone, and cancelling your Internet service. I do, however, want to provide you with some research-based facts about the content to which your children will be exposed—no matter how protective you are.

A few last things about me before we move on. Know that I am a father of four daughters, and a husband to a brilliant, beautiful woman. Know also that I consistently participate in media-related research. Because of my blog (ChildrenAndMediaMan.com), I constantly monitor the latest research so I can share it with parents and improve my own research. Although I may have a PhD in communication, like you I'm working on my PhD in parenting. I've found that my family type seems to be somewhat unique in academia. I've met many highly intelligent researchers. But I know very few who have as many kids as we do. So, I'd like to think that even though I may not be the smartest professor, and even though I've never given a TED Talk, I can see things a little differently because I view research through the lens of a parent of four kids. And because of that perspective, I view the media maze in an unconventional way, in a way that is practical and goes somewhat against the protective path that our media parenting normally takes.

Know also that the truth is, sometimes I feel like an overweight doctor telling patients that they need to lose weight. I let my kids view things that they probably shouldn't. My wife and I have very clear boundaries about media messages that have the potential to affect our children's developing feelings of self-worth. Yet on other things we're pretty lenient—we know virtually nothing about some of the games they play on the tablet, and we probably don't monitor what they do on their phones as often as we should. It's possible they've changed the passwords on their phones, and that they could have social media accounts that we don't know about. But, I hope through this book you'll see why we choose to guide our children's media exposure the way we do, with the understanding that our way may not be the best way for you and your children. Every family and every child is unique, so there is no single, clear-cut answer about how to direct your children's media exposure. But the research does provide us with some pretty clear conclusions about what messages the media sends, how media exposure affects our children, and what we can do about it.

It's important that you know that you have a stronger influence on your children than you think. Even though you don't have the map for the media maze—none of us do—we can empower our kids to make appropriate decisions when they encounter forks in the media road. While the change in focus from "protecting" to "empowering" our children may seem daunting at first, the fact that you are reading this book is proof enough that you are more than capable of helping your child navigate the Media Maze.

Notes

1. Nicholas Kardaras, "It's 'Digital Heroin': How Screens Turn Kids Into Psychotic Junkies," *New York Post,* August 27, 2016, http://nypost.com/2016/08/27/its-digital-heroin-how-screens-turn-kids-into-psychotic-junkies/.

2. Victoria Rideout, Ulla Foehr, and Donald Roberts, *Generation M²: Media in the Lives of 8- to 18-Year-Olds* (Menlo Park, CA: Kaiser Family Foundation, 2010), 1-79, https://kaiserfamilyfoundation.files.wordpress.com/2013/01/8010.pdf.

3. W. James Potter, *Media Literacy,* 7th ed., (London: SAGE, 2013), 4-5.

4. Steven Scott, *The Greatest Man Who Ever Lived* (Colorado Springs, CO: WaterBrook Press, 2009), 267.

# 2 The Media Maze

My favorite Harry Potter book is number four: *Harry Potter and the Goblet of Fire*. In the book, Harry competes in the Triwizard Tournament. For the tournament's last task, Harry and the other champions are required to seek the Triwizard Cup by navigating a maze full of lurking creatures and other obstacles. Harry's journey through the maze is full of attempted homicide, fantasy creatures, dark magic, and murder.

No matter how many times I read the book, something about the Triwizard maze captivates me. As soon as he enters the maze, Harry is shut off to the outside world. To save himself, all he has are his knowledge and his wit. He makes it as far as he can by himself, but we later learn that he reaches the end of the maze only because he has help. When we look at the maze through a media-parenting perspective, Harry's experience in the maze reveals some striking similarities between the dangers he faced and the dangers our kids face in today's media content. The dangers of media content are real, and like Harry in his maze, our children need help to navigate the media maze.

I'll admit, what you are about to read is a little hairy. I'm going to explain to you what you already suspect, and what you already worry about. After reading this chapter, you just might have the urge to never open this book again, lock your children up, and never let them watch TV or browse the Internet again. But hang in there with me. I'm going to do my best to present facts about children's media exposure without participating in the scaremongering that I dislike so much. So, while you read this chapter, keep in mind that we'll get to the good stuff—the solutions—a little later. In fact, this book is more about what you can do as a parent than it is about what content should concern us as parents. There is a way to the end of the maze, but we first need to know a bit about the maze.

Let's acknowledge first that despite what we often hear, not all media content is bad. I am as ardent a supporter of educational programming as perhaps Fred Rogers himself.[1] So, yes, good media exists. We'll touch on the good stuff in here also. But let's face it, most of the research about children and media exists because of the concerns of parents, educators, and policymakers about the potentially negative effect that media content has on children. Because of this, this book will lean toward focusing on what parents can do to help children avoid the effects of negative media content. And the picture painted by decades of research shows that the media maze is full of wrong turns and dead ends.

The Kaiser Family Foundation (KFF) is based in Menlo Park, California, not too far from Stanford University. A few years ago, the foundation issued a report called "Generation M[2]: Media in the Lives of 8- to 18-Year-Olds." The report describes the results of a nationwide survey of more than two thousand children in third to twelfth grade, and gives us a good picture of the amount of media to which our children are exposed. [2]

According to the report, the average American child between the ages of 8 and 18 consumes 7 hours and 38 minutes of media per day, 7 days a week. If you count using multiple media outlets at a time, such as watching TV and playing on the tablet at the same time, that number goes up to 10 hours and 45 minutes each day.

These numbers are especially significant because 5 years earlier, a similar study reported less media use. In fact, the KFF study found that over that 5-year period, children's exposure to music content increased by about 47 minutes. Exposure to TV increased by about 38 minutes, computer use was up 27 minutes, and kids played video games for about 24 more minutes every day. These numbers might surprise you—they surprised me. But here's the kicker: time spent reading decreased about 5 minutes per day.

A separate report documents the media lives of children ages 0–8.[3] As you'd expect, screen media use is much less than it is for older children. Kids under 2 years old spend about an hour each day with screen media. That goes up to about 2 hours each day for 2- to 4-year-olds and about 2 hours and 20 minutes daily for kids ages 5–8. In addition, time spent with mobile devices such as smart phones and tablets is on the rise. And just like with older children, time spent reading or being read to is on the decline.

Take a minute to pick your jaw up off the floor. Now take a deep breath. The KFF study involving older kids found that the main driver of the increase in much of this media use was mobile and online media. This shouldn't be too surprising knowing what you know about the advances and proliferation of smart phones, tablets, and bandwidth in recent years. For example, in 2004, I finally bought my first cell phone and upgraded from dial-up Internet for my home computer. I was more than happy to get rid of the eee-ooo-ooo-eee sound of the modem trying to connect. Seems like ages ago, doesn't it?

The age group that seems to spend the most time with media, according to the KFF report, are 11- to 14-year-olds. They spend, on average, about 8 hours and 40 minutes with media each day—about an hour more than the overall average. When you take media multitasking into account, that number jumps to nearly 12 hours per day, also about an hour more than average.[4]

Let's put these numbers into perspective. American children are spending just about the same amount of time or more during the day with media as they spend sleeping. In the school district where my family lives, children are required to be in school for about seven hours each day. If they sleep for eight hours a day, that means children spend all but one hour of their out-of-school time using media. Now, I understand that media consumption is a big part of our educational system and that some of that media time may occur in school, but the example serves as a valuable demonstration of how pervasive the media is in the lives of our children.

These media-use numbers are in stark contrast to the recommendations of policy groups such as the American Academy of Pediatrics (AAP). Led by medical doctor Jenny Radesky, a group of pediatricians and other researchers drafted a policy statement on behalf of the AAP in October 2016 that issued research-based guidelines about how much media children should be using. Here are a few highlights of their recommendations:

- Children younger than 18 months should only be allowed to use screen media for video chatting.
- Children ages 18 months to 2 years old should not watch any screen media that is not educational in nature.
- Children ages 2–5 should use screens for no more than 60 minutes per day.
- Children 6 and up should have clear boundaries for both the amount and type of media they are allowed to use.[5]

Notice that the recommendations—which I wholeheartedly endorse—refer to both media time and media content. It's clear that children, on average, spend far too much time using media. But what about media content? Just what are they seeing in those hours spent with screen media each day?

We'll start with what I call the "Big 4" types of media content that raise concern: violence, sex, substance use, and advertising. We can compare the Big 4 to dead ends or other dangers in the media maze—they make the media maze extremely difficult to navigate. We'll then briefly mention a few other types of media content including, fortunately, some of the good media content.

## Violence

First, let's define what we mean by media violence. Media violence refers to "aggressive actions that are likely to yield serious injury or death."[6] This definition encompasses a broad range of behaviors, from something as subtle as threatening to beat somebody up to more graphic depictions of murder.

The average American child views approximately 10,000 murders,[7] rapes, and aggravated assaults per year on TV. Assuming children wait to start watching TV until around age two (as the AAP recommends), that means by the time kids become teenagers, they have witnessed more than 100,000 murders, rapes, and aggravated assaults on TV.

A little more math reveals that if kids watch just over three hours of TV per day—and according to the KFF report, they do—that means for every hour they watch TV, they witness between nine and ten of these violent acts.

You might think that limiting children's exposure to just children's programming would change these numbers. However, research shows that children's shows actually contain *more* violence than adult shows: 7 out of 10 children's shows contain some violence, compared to 6 of 10 non-children's shows.[8] In addition, on children's TV, a violent act occurs once every 4 minutes, while in adult shows, violence occurs once every 12 minutes.[9]

True, violence in children's cartoons is probably less gory and graphic than violence in adult shows—watching Wile E. Coyote accidentally blow himself up with ACME TNT seems much more sanitized than seeing a character's brains being blown out of their head by an angry villain. But there are reasons why violence in children's programming may be just as harmful.

One of my favorite movies of all time is *The Incredibles*. My favorite character in the movie is Dash, or as his mother calls him, Dashiell Robert Parr. Dash is witty, likeable, and is portrayed as a boy with super talents who has to suppress some amazing attributes that make him feel special. The film has been praised for its action-packed focus on the family.[10]

In one scene, Dash and his sister, Violet, are discovered hiding in a tropical forest by the antagonists—the bad guys. In the ensuing few minutes, Dash uses his superhuman speed to try to outrun pilots chasing him in their disc-shaped flying machines.

When media scholars count the number of violent acts in a TV show or movie, they count each individual violent act. A punch, a bullet fired, a kick to the face. You may remember the scene where Dash runs across the water and hundreds of bullets smack the water just behind him as he runs away from the bad guys. Each one of those bullet strikes is considered an individual act of violence. You may also remember how fast Dash is able to punch one of the pilots over and over and over again. Again, each punch is considered its own act of violence. In this short sequence of events in *The Incredibles*, I'd wager there are several hundred, if not more than a thousand, acts of violence.

Three well-known scholars in the field of children and media—Drs. Victor Strasburger, Barbara Wilson, and Amy Jordan—reviewed all the research related to violence on TV and concluded that television violence, especially in children's programming, is problematic for several reasons.[11]

First, children conclude that violence in media is often justified because the good guys are often using violence for higher motives. For example, the Incredible family uses violence to take out Syndrome and his superhero-killing machine. Captain America uses violence to beat back enemies of the country. And hardly a crime show exists that doesn't show police officers using violence to thwart criminals. When violence is justified to get rid of or punish bad guys, these scholars worry that it could lead children to believe that it is okay to use violence to resolve problems, especially if they think their point of view is the "right" point of view.

Second, TV violence often goes unpunished. In fact, Dash's parents use violence right along with him! Violence is often rewarded in the media. For example, Moana and the demigod, Maui, are required to use violence in their quest to return the heart of Te Fiti to its rightful owner, and they are rewarded with a new hook and a magical healing of all the dying plants on the islands. These examples don't even begin to address the emotional toll that perpetrating violence takes on a person. TV simply doesn't accurately portray the realities of violence.

Third, media violence often results in no serious harm to the victim. How many times did Wile E. Coyote fall off a mile-high cliff into a cloud of dust below, but then get up again to try to blast the Road Runner with TNT? Often, instead of showing a victim in the final throes of death, they are instead seen sulking away in defeat, never to return.

Do you remember the scene in *Night at the Museum* when Larry the security guard and Dexter the monkey slap each other over and over again? That's one of my favorite movie scenes of all time. But the scene raises some concerns. First of all, some special interest group would go absolutely berserk if a video of me slapping a monkey ever came to light. Also, and related to the point I'm trying to make, I'm not the strongest guy, but if I did slap a monkey, I'm pretty sure the monkey would be unable to pick himself up off the floor with the strength to slap me back.

In another movie, *Tangled*, Flynn Rider and Maximus the horse fight each other over a stolen crown, kicking and clawing at each other until they accidentally fall off a cliff that is hundreds of feet high. Miraculously, they land gently on a soft bed of green grass and walk away from both the fight and the fall unharmed. Because TV's depiction of violence rarely reveals the consequences of violence for both the perpetrator and the victim, children may not understand its true effects.

This is precisely why parents should be concerned about media exposure. Living in the media maze almost guarantees exposure to media violence.

## Sexual Content

Now for some unsexy statistics about sexy media content. When we talk about sexual media content, we are talking about anything within the range of characters wearing tight or alluring clothing to sexual innuendos via images or words (or music) to actual depictions of people having sex. We will also be talking about pornography, which is considered by many researchers to be in a class by itself, even though some parents would consider a lingerie commercial to be pornography. Sexual media content hasn't always been an obvious obstacle in the media maze, but as we'll see, it has become an ever-present traveling companion to our children.

Research shows that about 75% of "prime time" shows on major TV networks contain what is considered to be sexual content. At the same time, just 14% of these shows mention anything about the risks or responsibilities of engaging in sexual behaviors.[12]

The term "prime time" here is significant because it refers to the evening hours when families are most likely to watch television. In fact, many parents agree that prime time television should contain content that is suitable for all audiences, including children.

Here are a few more numbers that may or may not surprise you: about 25% of all female characters in family films (G, PG, and PG-13) are depicted in sexy, tight, or alluring clothing.[13] About one-third of all popular rock songs contain sexual references,[14] and about 70% of teenagers have accidentally been exposed to pornography online.[15] That means that if you have a teenager in your family, it is likely that they have seen online pornography.

The prevalence of sex, sexy, and other sexual content on TV and in other media has led many scholars to agree that media, especially TV, has become perhaps the "leading sex educator" in our country.[16] Imagine that! Our children are learning about sex and what it means to be a sexual being from TV.

Now, I understand that when it comes to sex, you likely have a different belief system than me. But regardless of your belief system, researchers have analyzed the content of media programming and concluded that media depicts sex and sexual relationships in certain ways.[17]

For example, children learn from media that women are expected to look and act a certain way in order to be attractive to men. They are taught that it is socially acceptable for any two consenting adults—married to each other or not—to participate in a sexual or romantic relationship. They learn that the notions of mutual monogamy and waiting until marriage to have sex are outdated and old-fashioned.

Children also learn some higher-level sexual concepts, like just what it means to be a man or a woman. They learn to stereotype sexual minorities based on how they are portrayed in the media. Sex is also often associated with alcohol in the media.

Just like with violence, media rarely show the true consequences of recreational and unhealthy sexual behaviors. In real life, recreational sex is consistently linked to regret, loss of respect, embarrassment, and even depression, but media rarely shows these effects. Nor does it often show unplanned pregnancies or the transmission of sexually transmitted diseases.

Even children's shows are not immune to the portrayal of sexual content. Remember, the definition of sexual content includes tight or alluring clothes. Think of Disney princesses. Ariel is only sixteen but swims around wearing only seashells on her upper body. The regular, daily attire of Princess Jasmine, who is apparently only fifteen years old, exposes her midriff.

Like many children, my kids fell in love with the movie *Frozen*. (Yes, it's a cute movie. But I hope I never, ever, have to hear about how much snowmen like summer again.) Although I don't recall anything particularly "sexy" about the movie, many other parents do.

Common Sense Media is an organization that provides independent ratings of various kinds for different media from a developmental perspective. For *Frozen*, they provided ratings on its educational value, positive messages, positive role models, violence and scariness, sexy stuff, language, consumerism, and substance use. Let me share with you why they said *Frozen* contains "sexy stuff": "Princess Anna thinks that she's fallen in love with Prince Hans in just a few hours (after some flirting and exchanging of favorite things) and ends up accepting his proposal. Then she spends time really getting to know Kristoff and actually falls in love. Two kisses at the end of the movie. Queen Elsa wears a tight sparkly dress with a high slit. The trolls want Anna and Kristoff to get married."[18]

In that one paragraph alone, we see several messages that *Frozen* sends about love and relationships. *Frozen* suggests that love is nothing more than physical attraction and hitting on someone. It suggests marriage is something to be taken lightly and that one's affections are allowed to change in a short period of time. It encourages the allure of tight, revealing clothing. And, of course, that every triumph requires physical affection.

These concerns may not sound like a big deal to you, and I empathize. I know I didn't get those messages from the show when I watched it. But concern exists that children's young minds will begin to piece together messages from this and all the other media they watch to form an overall picture of what sex and love mean.

Even seemingly innocuous, funny films, such as the *Minions* movie in 2015, contain sexual content. Here's what Common Sense Media had to say about *Minions*: "Glimpses of bare/thonged Minion bottom. Three Tower of London guards are hypnotized to strip down to their boxers and dance/ sing to the song "Hair," slapping each other on the behind. Additional innuendo related to Minions cozying up to some fire hydrants, losing a bathing suit (and covering up with sea life), squeezing bottoms, and staring at the chest of a group of Minions disguised to look like a woman."[19]

Funny? Sure. Is this a message we want to send to our children about appropriate relational behavior? Probably not.

## Pornography

Most of our discussion about sexual media content so far has focused on sexual content in what many consider to be popular, mainstream media. However, the prevalence of pornography in the lives of adolescents requires us to also consider it as mainstream. Indeed, pornography is scattered all across the walls of the media maze.

Research shows that millions of pornographic websites exist[20] and that about one-fourth of all search engine queries are for pornographic content.[21] One estimate suggests that in a recent 7.5-month period, pornography was searched for more than one billion times worldwide.[22]

Pornography exposure is widespread among adolescents. About 90% of boys are exposed to pornography before they reach adulthood, and on average, they first see pornography around age twelve.[23]

Concern exists about children's exposure to pornography because of the messages it contains. One study found that nearly 90% of best-selling pornography videos contained physical and verbal aggression in association with sex, including spanking, gagging, and name-calling.[24] Pornography often dehumanizes and devalues women and places them in subordination to men.

While there is a small body of research that states some adults think viewing pornography is beneficial to their sexual health,[25] there is no research—absolutely none—that concludes pornography is in any way beneficial to children.

Before I conclude this section, I want to share a personal experience about exposure to sexual content. I was twelve or thirteen years old, right at the age when heterosexual boys are getting interested in girls and when puberty starts to do strange things to the body. Our family must have had a subscription to *Sports Illustrated*, because I saw it one day when I went out to the mailbox. It was the swimsuit issue.

Thinking that if my parents thought it was okay to subscribe to the magazine, then it must be okay for me to look at, I took the magazine up to my bedroom. Now, many people don't consider the *SI* swimsuit issue to be pornographic. But researchers often define pornography as any media "construed as intended to entertain or arouse erotic desire."[26] Under that definition, the swimsuit issue can be classified as pornography. I mean, they're not presenting the pictures to a primarily male readership with the hopes of selling swimsuits, right? The intent is obvious.

So, on this day, I took the magazine up to my room, and as any typical heterosexual teenage boy would be, I was pretty fascinated. Now, let me just say that if my parents had known that their pubescent son would get his hands on this magazine, they would have cancelled their subscription without a second thought.

After about ten minutes of looking at the magazine, I started to feel guilty. What I was doing was contrary to everything my parents had taught me. I had been taught that a woman's body was to be respected, and nothing I saw in the magazine seemed to jive with that.

Looking back, I can see now how even just a few minutes of exposure to what many don't consider pornography altered my reasoning. I wanted to hide the magazine. I wanted to throw it away. I began to think of the best way to cover my tracks.

I could throw it away, but what if my parents found it in the garbage? They would know that someone had looked at it. I could take it outside and burn it, but if they found the ashes, they'd know that I had looked at it.

For some reason, I figured that the best place to hide the magazine so my parents would never know I saw it was underneath the bucket of laundry detergent in the laundry room. I figured that the bucket of detergent would never go dry—it was bought at Costco, and whatever is bought at Costco lasted forever.

Ironically, of all the places I could dispose of the magazine, my erroneous reasoning led me to put it in the one place that would guarantee my mom found it. About a week later, I snuck into the laundry room to make sure nobody had found the magazine, and it was gone.

To this day, my decision to hide the magazine under the laundry detergent stumps me. It seems evident that my exposure to those pictures altered my reasoning to the point that I could not reason my way through how to dispose of the magazine.

I've learned since then that the brain has an amazing capacity to retain memories (we'll get to a bunch of brain research in the last chapter), and the pictures in my mind won't ever be erased. However, they do serve as a good reminder to me of how easy it is for children to find objectionable sexual content.

To illustrate how easy it is for kids to find sexual content, we need look no further than the burger joint Carl's Jr. In a move touted as a moral awakening for the company, Carl's Jr. announced in March 2017 that leather bikinis and nearly naked women would no longer be a part of their burger advertising strategy.

Normally, I'd jump for joy at such news. But digging into the situation, we learn a bit more about the reasons for the sudden moral turnaround. Advertising consultants for the parent company of Carl's Jr. and Hardees said it was "time to evolve" away from its edgy branding in order to direct focus back on its food.[27] *The Washington Post* reported, however, that according to a company executive, the real reason for dumping the sexy ads was because "young, hungry guys aren't as affected by the racy ads with the swimsuit models because you can get a lot of that on the internet now."[28]

In other words, the young, male demographic targeted by the racy ads has become so desensitized to sex because of the amount of pornography available online, that the sex in Carl's Jr.'s commercials just wasn't having the same effect anymore (see a discussion about desensitization in the last chapter of this book).

At this point, it would seem appropriate to jump right in and start talking about the effects of exposure to sexual and violent content. We'll get there, I promise. But first, let's spend a few more minutes reviewing the other types of media content that serve as wrong turns in the media maze.

## Substance Use

Take ten seconds and answer the following question. Ready? How many US presidents can you name? Let's see: George Washington, John Adams, Thomas Jefferson, Abraham Lincoln, Richard Nixon, Jimmy Carter, Ronald Reagan, Bill Clinton, George Bush #1, George Bush #2, Barack Obama, and Donald Trump. That's twelve, not bad.

The average American child between the ages of 8 and 12 can name 4 American presidents. In isolation, that's not too bad—that will probably get them through most history tests and maybe even the SAT. These same children, however, can name 5 brands of beer.[29] Said differently, kids can name 25% more beer brands than they can US presidents.

Drugs, alcohol, and tobacco are splattered across the media. The average American youth sees about two thousand alcohol ads on TV each year.[30] In fact, teenagers see more tobacco and alcohol advertising than adults.[31]

On average, about 75% of the top 100 movies at the box office contain smoking,[32] and about 1 in 3 of the top prime-time TV shows feature alcohol. About 81% of middle and high schoolers have seen smoking in TV or in movies.[33] About 22% of movies contain depictions of illicit drugs, and more than half of these show no harmful consequences of using illicit drugs.[34]

In one study looking at the Facebook profiles of an all-male undergraduate sample, researchers found that 85% of profiles contained some kind of reference to alcohol.[35] And in a national study involving nearly 800 US teenagers (ages 13–17), 29.7% of them said they recalled seeing alcohol advertising online in the past 30 days, compared to 16.8% of adults.[36]

You might be like me when I first heard these numbers. They were hard to believe. It's also hard to believe that *any* children's programming would contain alcohol and tobacco. But each of the following children's programs or movies shows characters smoking: *Aladdin, Hercules, Tom & Jerry, Rango, 101 Dalmatians, Pinocchio, Peter Pan, The Flintstones, Dumbo, Alice in Wonderland*, and *The Hunchback of Notre Dame*, to name a few.

Additionally, the following movies are examples of children's movies that show, talk about, or allude to alcohol: *Sleeping Beauty, Brave, Beauty and the Beast, Dumbo, Peter Pan, The Hunchback of Notre Dame, Fantasia, Tangled* (remember the Snuggly Duckling tavern?), and *The Great Mouse Detective.*

I think that's enough data to scare you. However, as I said before, I don't want reading this book to be an exercise in fear. My intent in sharing this information is to make you aware of the content to which your kids will most likely be exposed.

Much of the alcohol use to which children are exposed comes in the form of advertising. But, in addition to the quantity of ads containing portrayals of substance use, what concerns me and other scholars about alcohol and tobacco in the media is how they are portrayed.[37]

Alcohol is nearly always portrayed in association with young, attractive actors. I recently saw a beer commercial that started with two fully clothed men sitting at an outdoor bar at the beach. Two blonde women in bikinis walk up to the bar, and the scene shifts to the guys kicking off their shoes, two other women in bikinis kicking off their shoes, and many other attractive men and women kicking off their shoes.

The commercial ends with a guy sitting in a beach chair, holding a beer, while two women in bikinis walk toward him. We don't see the women's faces, only their butts and their legs. In the commercial, I counted twelve women in bikinis and eight fully clothed yet thin and attractive women.

In another recent beer commercial, I found it interesting that the primary female actors, all of whom were fully clothed, faced the camera. But the women who wore bikinis were either facing away from the camera—with a focus on their backsides—or their faces were blurred by the camera. Such a commercial typifies the portrayal of alcohol in the media. It seems to always be associated with sex in one way or another.

The portrayal of alcohol and tobacco on TV makes it seem like everyone drinks and smokes, and that smoking and drinking will lead to fun, sex, and parties. Not to mention wealth—have you noticed how those parties seem to always be on the top of high rises in the city or on the beach?

Maybe smoking and drinking do, in fact, lead to fun, sex, parties, and wealth. But that's not the issue. The issue is that tobacco and alcohol are illegal and unhealthy for children, and the companies that produce these products are engaging in practices that deceive children about the merits, benefits, and risks of consuming them. In this way, alcohol advertising is one of the trickiest paths to navigate in the media maze.

## Advertising

Name the brand associated with the slogan "Just do it." Of course, Nike. Now, "Melts in your mouth, not in your hands." Right, M&Ms. How about "The happiest place on earth"? Right again, Disneyland. Now, name the Speaker of the House—the person who will become president of the

United States if something were to happen to both the president and vice president. That one is a bit harder, isn't it? We have advertising to blame. (By the way, in 2017 the Speaker of the House was Paul Ryan.)

The average American child sees about 25,000 advertisements each year.[38] That's a whopping 68 advertisements *every day*! Likely as a result, when it comes to product purchases, children choose brand-name products over nonbrand-name products nearly 70% of the time.[39] And only 3% of advertisements aimed at children are for healthy food.[40]

Seventeen billion dollars a year is spent on advertising to children.[41] Most of these advertisements are for cereal, candy, toys, and fast-food restaurants. Advertising comes in many forms. A popular form in recent years is product placements.

One of my least favorite movies ever, *Castaway*, is the first movie I can recall that included a form of product placement. The inclusion of the FedEx brand is a prominent part of the movie's plot and a good example of a product placement. More recently, Legos are a not-so-subtle part of *The Lego Movie* plot.

Maybe big-screen product placements don't bother you too much. Perhaps that's because they've become so commonplace. Product placements have become a typical element in reality shows—consider *The Biggest Loser*. When they make food in the kitchen, the camera always seems to zoom in on a brand name. That's not by chance.

Products are even placed in media designed specifically for children. A little bit of digging on the Internet revealed the following book titles: *Skittles Riddles Math*, *The Hershey Kisses Addition Book*, and *The Cheerios Christmas Play Book*.

Product placements are also found in video games. According to cracked.com, the game *Metal Gear Solid: Peace Walker* features Doritos, Pepsi, Mountain Dew, and Axe Body Spray.[42] Chupa Chupa Lollipops are found in *Zool: Ninja of the Nth Dimension*. Car brands are featured in enough video games that some have called the relationship between video-game makers and the auto industry a $2.8 billion dollar "symbiotic relationship."[43]

Cross-promotional advertising is a term describing the connection of two different products in some way. Perhaps the best-known example of a company that engages in cross-promotion is McDonald's and their Happy Meal tie-ins. A website called "Happy Meal Toys Collection Fan Site" contains lists of McDonalds's cross-promotions for Harper Books, *The SpongeBob Movie*, Hot Wheels, Barbie, Transformers, Nerf, Minions, *The Lego Movie*, Pokémon, Madden NFL, Littlest Pet Shop, Flutterbye Fairy, and many more.[44] Some estimates suggest that the 1.5 billion toys distributed annually by McDonald's makes it the largest toy distributor in the United States.[45]

Children are exposed to so much advertising that even at a young age they are able to identify which consumer products belong to which brand. For example, in one study involving 196 kids ages 2–8, researchers found that 2-year-olds were able to associate nearly 8 of 12 consumer products with the correct brand.[46] And 8-year-olds could do the same for nearly all the products/brands in the study.[47]

Children are also exposed to excessive amounts of online advertising. One study showed that 87% of popular children's websites contain advertising of some kind.[48]

Online advertising is a different beast than television or print advertising. The Internet, due to its very nature, is interactive. This means that children can interact with brands, getting more face time with them, and become more attached to them. And with the rise of cookies, online advertisers can send targeted advertisements based on what they know about the demographics and search patterns of the user.

Even banner ads are still used online. A Yale University study found that more than three billion banner ads for food and drinks were viewed on children's websites during a recent one-year period.[49]

In addition, I spoke with one parent recently whose child racked up more than $600 in in-app purchases on the day he got his new tablet. Online advertising is everywhere, and it seems to draw children in.

I suppose there is nothing inherently wrong with advertising—without it, we wouldn't know what movies are playing at the theater, what new products might help us communicate with each other better, and what new drug might help ease a chronic health condition (despite a long list of potential horrific side effects). Advertising plays an important informational purpose in our society.

But when it comes to kids, the rules change. It takes time for children to develop the skills necessary to critically analyze advertisements. Children are less able to distinguish fiction from reality and advertising from other media content. This means that they are more prone to believe things they see on TV. If Red Bull gives you wings, children may at first believe that they will magically sprout wings if they drink it.

Children are less able to perceive that something is trying to persuade them. Without that ability, they are unable to bring up mental arguments that might run contrary to the information in an advertisement. These, and other deficits in cognitive development, make children more susceptible to the influences of advertising, effects that we'll talk about in the next chapter.

## Video Games

Now that we've discussed the Big 4 types of media content that cause concern, let's talk about some other types of media that parents worry about.

It seems like whenever there is a high-profile act of violence, people immediately jump to the conclusion that American children are playing far too many video games. In reality, the average American child spends far less time playing video games than watching TV or listening to music.

According to the Kaiser Family Foundation study, the average 8- to 18-year-old in this country spends about 1 hour and 13 minutes each day playing video games on a video console, handheld video game player, or cell phone. These numbers compare to about 4.5 hours that children spend watching TV each day, time that consists of watching live TV, on-demand TV, self-recorded TV, DVDs, and shows on other devices like the Internet and cell phones.[50] Boys, perhaps not surprisingly, spend far more time with video games than girls.[51]

If the time children spent playing video games was devoted to educational pursuits, this section would be full of positive information. While I recognize the potential good that video games can have (how would I have learned about the Oregon Trail without the video game?), the truth is that most kids are not spending a majority of their time using video games in order to improve their intelligence. Concern exists about children's video game use because of video games' portrayals of violence, sexuality, and female body imagery.

I'd like to first share the results of a study about how women's bodies are portrayed in video games, followed by gender and sexuality portrayals, and finally violence in video games.

The study was led by Dr. Nicole Martins, a children and media scholar who is highly respected among those in our field.[52] She and her colleagues gathered the top 150 video games across the 9 major gaming systems that were sold in the US in a recent 1-year period, including Xbox, PlayStation, and Nintendo systems. They recorded an expert game player playing each game for 30 minutes, then reviewed the recordings and compared the bodies of video-game women to those of real women. For sake of comparison, they transformed each of the measurements so that they applied to a woman about 5 feet 4 inches tall.[53]

In every way, the video-game characters were different than the average American woman. The video-game women adhered to the thin ideal found in media. Women in video games had larger heads, smaller chests, smaller waists, and smaller hips than the typical American woman. The women in the highly realistic video games were also smaller compared to video-game women in nonrealistic games who were the same height.

In other words, women who were displayed more realistically and with more detail tended to conform more to the thin ideal that is so often seen in media, rather than the women in the less detailed video games. The study also compared games that were considered children's games to games considered as adult games. They found that children's games portrayed females as having smaller chests, smaller waists, and smaller hips than adult games did.

What this study shows is that, like TV and other mainstream media, video games tend to show women as thinner than the average woman. We call this the thin-ideal standard—a standard of beauty that is highly unrealistic and highly unattainable for most women. Specifically, the study found that the average video-game female is 5 feet 4 inches tall, has a 29-inch bust, a 22-inch waist, and 31-inch hips.[54] Women, does this sound attainable to you? Men, it's possible that we will never meet a woman that looks like the average video-game woman.

Men and women are portrayed differently in video games, as you might suspect. For example, in a study that looked at the top sixty best-selling console video games, male characters appear more frequently than female characters in video games.[55] And when female characters did appear, they were much more likely than male characters to be depicted wearing revealing clothing, partially or fully nude, and with an unrealistic body type.[56]

Another study looked at the introductory videos of twelve popular video games. Half of the games featured female leading characters and half featured male leading characters. As you might expect by now, most female characters were portrayed with large breasts (think Lara Croft) and "eye catching" and "difficult to ignore" buttocks.[57]

Beyond the interest in video games' portrayals of women, gender, and sexuality, more attention has been paid over the years to violence in video games. One of the first larger studies to look at the amount of violence in video games was conducted in 1989[58] and looked at arcade games.[59] The study defined video game violence as "the act of destroying individuals or objects or the ingestion of individuals." Yes, you read that right: "The ingestion of individuals." I don't know exactly what that means outside of Pac Man swallowing a ghost, but it doesn't sound like it would be particularly enjoyable for a human victim. The study found that nearly 75% of the most popular video games contained such violence.

Another study analyzing home gaming systems found that nearly 80% of the most popular home video games contained aggression, and 21% contained some sort of violence against women.[60]

Yet another study found that nearly 70% of 60 of the most popular games on 3 home gaming systems contained violence.[61] In that study, a researcher played each game for 10 minutes. The study found that games rated as appropriate for adults contained 4.59 acts of violence per minute, and that games rated as appropriate for kids contained 1.17 acts of violence per minute.

That means that if a child plays video games for an average of 73 minutes per day, as mentioned above, it is likely that they are exposed to—or even virtually enact themselves—somewhere between 85 and 335 acts of violence each day!

Another study looked at video games that can be played on personal computers.[62] Again, a professional gamer was recorded while playing each of 20 top-selling games for 10–30 minutes. About 60% of these games included violence as a major theme of the game, and about half of these violent games were presented from the viewpoint of the perpetrator of the violence.

While video games don't necessarily introduce content of concern that isn't already found in other media, concern exists due to how the interactive nature of video games combines with an elevated prevalence of violence, sex, and unrealistic female body imagery.

## Internet/Social Media

Can you believe we've covered so much ground and have hardly even touched on the Internet yet? Statistics for how much time youth spend using the Internet and social media are hard to pin down. In the past, a desktop or laptop computer was required in order to access the Internet; now, a multitude of handheld devices will do the trick.

There used to be a clear separation in what you could do with specific media. For example, the only way to watch TV used to be to turn on the TV. Now, kids can watch TV online, anytime.

When I was a kid, I would read the sports section of the local newspaper over breakfast in the morning. I loved the feel of the newspaper in my hands. Now, I read almost all my news online because I don't have to pay a subscription fee to access the content. Music is accessed online, not just on a CD player or MP3 player. In other words, the Internet is so interactive that it is hard to quantify just how much time kids are spending online and what activities they are doing.

Here is some of what we do know. About 90% of American and European youth ages 12 to 17 spend at least some time using the Internet every day.[63] Nearly one-third of kids under the age of 8 spend time daily with tablets, smart phones, and other devices that would be considered "new media." More than half of kids ages 2–4 have used a computer before.[64] When my youngest daughter was in kindergarten, she knew how to access pbskids.org and play games that I had never played.

I don't believe there is anything inherently wrong with the Internet. In fact, my life and the lives of my family members have been enhanced in countless ways because of the Internet. Our kids have access to news about current events. They can find information about lemurs in Madagascar without digging through an outdated encyclopedia. They can communicate with their friends. My kids can talk face-to-face with both sets of grandparents—who each live about 1,500 miles away—because of video chat capabilities of the Internet. We do much of our shopping online.

I don't need to list all the benefits of the Internet. You know them, and you want your kids to enjoy them. But access to any kind of information online also has its risks. You know that too. You worry and agonize about that. Without trying to scare you, here is a bit of information about potential Internet risks that has been a focus of research in my field.

Though numbers vary by study, one study involving a nationally representative sample of 1,501 youth found that about 20% of youth ages 10–17 were sexually solicited online, and within the past year, about 25% of these kids accidentally viewed pictures of naked people or of people having sex.[65] Another study found that nearly 90% of the most popular children's websites include advertising of some sort,[66] and even though it's prohibited by the Children's Online Privacy Protection Act, nearly 75% of children's websites collect children's personal information.[67] About 10% of teens have sent a sext (either text or image), and about 16% have received a sext.[68] As you know, these statistics are just a few of the potentially negative things kids could encounter online. Without a doubt, the Internet may be the most confusing and troubling part of the media maze.

## Educational/Prosocial Content

Sometimes we focus so much on the bad media content that we forget that an ample amount of good content is out there. So parents, take heart. Not all media content will ruin your kids. In fact, despite the pessimism that you may have felt reading this chapter so far, you should know that I'm optimistic about the potential for good media to help our kids learn and develop skills that they might otherwise not obtain. And I'm encouraged by research showing that some children seem to be spending a significant portion of their daily media time with educational videos.

For example, one study found that many US preschoolers spend on average about 55 minutes each day watching educational programming.[69] Just what is educational programming, you ask? Researchers recently explored that very question. One study looked at 15 programs that met at least one of the following criteria: (1) they were funded at least in part by the US Department of Education's Ready to Learn program, (2) they included language and literacy content and were aired on a PBS station, or (3) they were rated by Nielsen as a top-rated program for preschoolers.[70]

The list of shows in the study included *Super Why, Martha Speaks, Between the Lions, Sesame Street, Word World, Arthur & Friends, Clifford the Big Red Dog, Reading Rainbow, Barney & Friends, WordGirl, Blue's Clues, Dora the Explorer, Go Diego Go, Franklin & Friends*, and *Curious George*. I should note here that because of the length of time that it takes to conduct and publish a study, the list is missing at least four really good educational programs that have since become quite popular: *Daniel Tiger's Neighborhood, Peg + Cat, Odd Squad*, and *Wild Kratts*.

One important characteristic of the programs in the study was that each had specific instructional goals—a key attribute of media that can be described as "educational." Common goals of educational media include improving children's literacy skills (such as letter identification and letter-sound correspondence), language development (such as vocabulary), prosocial development (such as development of friendships and of social and emotional skills), and general skills development (such as knowledge about math, animals, or science). The study looked at all the shows and found that the most common type of learning goal is the acquisition of language skills, followed by prosocial skills, general skills, and finally, literacy skills.

Let me remind you here that I'm a parent first and researcher second. While it's interesting to know what type of content is considered "educational," what this really tells me as a parent is that some TV time is okay. Like most parents, sometimes I use screens as a babysitter. In order to get anything done, sometimes we have to plop our kids in front of the TV or pull up a video on the tablet.

I think a lot of parents feel guilty about doing this. But, don't we get enough parenting guilt? I'm increasingly convinced, based on the research I've conducted and seen, that although we lament the state of media content, we have some really good options to choose from in those moments when we just need half an hour to clean the kitchen or to just waste time on social media. Yes, our primary reason for using media may be to distract our kids, but it can actually be a win-win for parents: we can take great advantage of this needed "alone" time while our kids watch programming that helps supplement what we and their school teachers are trying to teach them.

## Conclusion

We've talked a lot in this chapter about the different types of media content children are viewing, and we haven't really even scratched the surface. However, I hope that after reading this chapter you have a better idea of what content is out there and how much time the average child is viewing that content.

I don't know of any better way to describe what our children face today than by calling it a "media maze." I know that some of the media in this maze is pretty scary, and I also know we didn't spend nearly enough time on the positive media choices available to kids. However, there is a reason we spent so much time going over the risks associated with media use—simply stated, I don't think we as parents can properly deal with the risks unless we know what they are.

The way I see it, there are three ways to deal with the problem of negative media content and the staggering amounts of time our children spend with this content.

First, we could lock our kids up and hide them away from the world—we could try to keep them from using media in the first place. But in the words of Dory on the movie *Finding Nemo*, "Well, you can't never let anything happen to him. Then, nothing would ever happen to him." Children would miss out on the good if we protect them too much from the bad.

Second, we could advocate for and impose regulations and restrictions on media content. We could let the government decide what is and isn't appropriate for our children and enforce laws to ensure compliance. We could let the government determine how much violence is too much, what defines obscenity, and how much screen time is too much for our kids.

On the surface, if government regulations regulated media content in a way that would ensure that our children were never exposed to certain content in the first place, our lives would be much easier. Personally, though, the idea of censorship makes me feel uncomfortable. If special interest groups could convince lawmakers to censor violent TV content, they could also convince them to censor religious content and content that many consider to be consistent with family values. Considering where society is today, it doesn't seem like that far of a leap to believe that one day our special-interest-driven government could enact media laws that severely restrict everyone's freedom to watch and create media content of their choice. If you ask me, I think it's better to have no censorship than to have any censorship at all—it just feels American, and right, to limit censorship instead of limiting media content. I'd rather have the bad with the good than to not have the good at all. So, option two is off the table.

Option three puts the responsibility of dealing with media content squarely on the shoulders of parents. That seems like the best option to me, albeit the most difficult to personally enforce. Therefore, in the next two chapters, we will discuss some of the research that shows how exposure to all the media content we've talked about so far affects children's well-being. After that, we'll get to the meat of the book and learn about the powerful role parents can play in altering the media's influence on children.

## Notes

1. As a gift once, I was even given a mug with a picture of Fred Rogers on it. When the liquid inside the mug gets hot, Fred magically changes from wearing a suit coat to wearing a cardigan sweater. It sits on my office shelf next to a plush Daniel Tiger doll, who also happens to be wearing a red cardigan. Best swag I've ever received.

2. Victoria Rideout, Ulla Foehr, and Donald Roberts, *Generation M²: Media in the Lives of 8- to 18-Year-Olds* (Menlo Park, CA: Kaiser Family Foundation, 2010), 1-79, https://kaiserfamilyfoundation.files.wordpress.com/2013/01/8010.pdf.

3. Victoria Rideout, *Zero to Eight: Children's Media Use in America 2013* (San Francisco, CA: Common Sense Media, 2013), 1-38, www.commonsensemedia.org/research/zero-to-eight-childrens-media-use-in-america-2013.

4. Victoria Rideout, *Generation M²: Media in the Lives of 8- to 18-Year-Olds*, 1-79.

5. AAP Council on Communications and Media, "Media and Young Minds," *Pediatrics* 138, no. 5 (2016): doi: 10.1542/peds.2016-2591.

6. Craig Anderson, Brad Bushman, Edward Donnerstein, Tom Hummer, and Wayne Warburton, "SPSSI Research Summary on Media Violence," *The Society for the Psychological Study of Social Issues*, April 2014, http://www.spssi.org/index.cfm?fuseaction=page.viewPage&pageID=1899&nodeID=1.

7. Aletha Huston et al., *Big World, Small Screen: The Role of Television in American Society* (Lincoln: University of Nebraska Press, 1992), 54.

8. Barbara Wilson et al., "Violence in Children's Television Programming: Assessing the Risks," *Journal of Communication* 52, no. 1 (2002): 5-35.

9. For a review, see also Victor Strasburger, Barbara Wilson, and Amy Jordan, *Children, Adolescents, and the Media*, 3rd ed., (Thousand Oaks, CA: Sage, 2014).

10. "The Incredibles Movie Review," *Common Sense Media*, accessed May 24, 2017, https://www.commonsensemedia.org/movie-reviews/the-incredibles.

11. Strasburger, Wilson, and Jordan, *Children, Adolescents, and the Media*, 133-194.

12. Dale Kunkel et al., *Sex on TV 4: A Biennial Report to the Kaiser Family Foundation* (Menlo Park CA: Kaiser Family Foundation, 2005), 38, https://kaiserfamilyfoundation.files.wordpress.com/2013/01/sex-on-tv-4-full-report.pdf.

13. Stacy Smith and Marc Choueiti, *Gender Disparity on Screen and Behind the Camera in Family Films: An Executive Summary* (Los Angeles, CA: Geena Davis Institute on Gender in Media, 2010), 2.

14. Brian Primack et al., "Degrading and Non-degrading Sex in Popular Music: A Content Analysis," *Public Health Reports* 123, no. 5 (2008): 593-600, doi: 10.1177/003335490812300509.

15. Victoria Rideout, *Generation RX.com: How Young People Use the Internet for Health Information* (Menlo Park, CA: Kaiser Family Foundation, 2001), 12, https://kaiserfamilyfoundation.files.wordpress.com/2001/11/3202-genrx-report.pdf.

16. Victor Strasburger, "Adolescents, Sex, and the Media: Ooooo, Baby, Baby—A Q&A," *Adolescent Medicine Clinics* 16, no. 2 (2005): 269, doi: 10.1016/j.admecli.2005.02.009.

17. Strasburger, Wilson, and Jordan, *Children, Adolescents, and the Media*, 195-270.

18. *Frozen* movie review, *Common Sense Media,* accessed May 24, 2017, https://www.commonsensemedia.org/movie-reviews/frozen-0.

19. *Minions* movie review, *Common Sense Media,* accessed May 24, 2017, https://www.commonsensemedia.org/movie-reviews/minions.

20. Milton Diamond, "Pornography, Public Acceptance and Sex Related Crime: A Review," *International Journal of Law and Psychiatry* 32, no. 5 (2009), 304-314, doi: 10.1016/j.ijlp.2009.06.004.

21. Al Cooper, David Delmonico, and Ron Burg, "Cybersex Users, Abusers, and Compulsives: New Findings and Implications," *Sexual Addiction and Compulsivity* 7, no. 1-2 (2000): 5-29, doi: 10.1080/10720160008400205.

22. "Pornography Statistics," *Covenant Eyes,* accessed June 21, 2017, http://www.covenanteyes.com/pornstats/.

23. Ibid.

24. Ana Bridges et al., "Aggression and Sexual Behavior in Best-Selling Pornography Videos: A Content Analysis Update," *Violence Against Women* 16, no. 10 (2010): 1065-1085, doi: 10.1177/1077801210382866.

25. Gert Hald and Neil Malamuth, N. M., "Self-Perceived Effects of Pornography Consumption," *Archives of Sexual Behavior* 37, no 4 (2008): 614-625, doi: 10.1007/s10508-007-9212-1.

26. Milton Diamond, "Pornography, Public Acceptance and Sex Related Crime: A Review," 304.

27. Madeline Farber, "Carl's Jr. Has a New Ad and This One Doesn't Have Girls in Bikinis," *Fortune,* March 30, 2017, http://fortune.com/2017/03/30/carls-jr-new-ad-sans-bikini/.

28. Abha Bhattarai, "Carl's Jr.: Sex No Longer Sells," *The Washington Post*, March 30, 2017, https://www.washingtonpost.com/news/business/wp/2017/03/30/carls-jr-sex-no-longer-sells/?utm_term=.8a2075a3039c.

29. Center for Science in the Public Interest, *Kids Are as Aware of Booze as Presidents, Survey Finds* (Washington, DC: Center for Science in the Public Interest, 1988), quoted in Victor Strasburger, Barbara Wilson, and Amy Jordan, *Children, Adolescents, and the Media*, 3rd ed., (Thousand Oaks, CA: SAGE, 2014), 92.

30. Council on Communications and Media, "Policy Statement—Children, Adolescents, Substance Abuse, and the Media," *Pediatrics* 126, no. 4 (2010): 791-799, doi: 10.1542/peds.2010-1635.

31. Center on Alcohol Marketing and Youth, *Youth Exposure to Alcohol Advertising on Television, 2001-2009.* (Baltimore, MD: Johns Hopkins School of Public Health, 2010), 1-3, http://www.camy.org/_docs/resources/reports/youth-exposure-alcohol-advertising-tv-01-09-exec-sum.pdf.

32. James Sargent, Susanne Tanski, and Jennifer Gibson, "Exposure to Movie Smoking Among US Adolescents Aged 10 to 14 years: A Population Estimate," *Pediatrics* 119, no. 5 (2007): doi: 10.1542/peds.2006-2897.

33. Jennifer Duke et al., "Reported Exposure to Pro-Tobacco Messages in the Media: Trends Among Youth in the United States, 2000-2004," *American Journal of Health Promotion* 23, no. 3 (2009): 195-202, doi: 10.4278/ajhp.071130126.

34. Donald Roberts and Peter Christenson, *"Here's Looking at You, Kid": Alcohol, Drugs and Tobacco in Entertainment Media: A Literature Review Prepared for The National Center on Addiction and Substance Abuse at Columbia University* (Menlo Park, CA: Kaiser Family Foundation, 2000), 1-40. http://files.eric.ed.gov/fulltext/ED443062.pdf.

35. Katie Egan and Megan Moreno, "Alcohol References on Undergraduate Males' Facebook Profiles," *American Journal of Men's Health* 5, no. 5 (2011): 413-420, doi: 10.1177/1557988310394341. https://www.ncbi.nlm.nih.gov/pmc/articles/PMC3210384/.

36. David Jernigan et al., "Self-Reported Youth and Adult Exposure to Alcohol Marketing in Traditional and Digital Media: Results of a Pilot Survey," *Alcoholism Clinical and Experimental Research* 41, no. 3 (2017): 618-625, doi: 10.1111/acer.13331.

37. Strasburger, Wilson, and Jordan, "Children, Adolescents, and the Media," 271-336.

38. Walter Gantz, Nancy Schwartz, James Angelini, and Victoria Rideout, *Food for Thought: Television Food Advertising to Children in the United States* (Menlo Park, CA: Kaiser Family Foundation, 2007), 1-55, https://kaiserfamilyfoundation.files.wordpress.com/2013/01/7618.pdf.

39. Karen Pine and Avril Nash, "Barbie or Betty? Preschool Children's Preference for Branded Products and Evidence for Gender-Linked Differences," *Journal*

*of Developmental and Behavioral Pediatrics* 24, no. 4 (2003): 219-224, doi: 10.1097/00004703-200308000-00001.

40. Dale Kunkel and Walter Gantz, "Children's Television Advertising in the Multichannel Environment," *Journal of Communication* 42, no. 3 (1992): 134-152, doi: 10.111/j.1460-2466.1922.tb00803.x.

41. Christine Lagorio, "Resources: Marketing to Kids," *CBS News*, May 14, 2017, http://www.cbsnews.com/news/resources-marketing-to-kids/.

42. Andrew Heaton, "The 5 Least Subtle Product Placements in Gaming History," *Cracked*, February 20, 2014, http://www.cracked.com/article_20879_the-5-least-subtle-product-placements-in-gaming-history.html.

43. Christiaan Hetzner and Harro Ten Wolde, "Putting Cars in Video Games is Now a $2.8 Billion Industry," *Huffington Post*, August 22, 2013, http://www.huffingtonpost.com/2013/08/22/car-in-video-games_n_3793607.html.

44. "Happy Meal Toys: Fan Site," *Toys Affair*, accessed August 2, 2017, http://hm.toysaffair.com/.

45. Julian Barnes, "Fast-Food Giveaway Toys Face Rising Recalls," *The New York Times*, August 16, 2001, http://www.nytimes.com/2001/08/16/business/fast-food-giveaway-toys-face-rising-recalls.html.

46. Patti Valkenburg and Moniek Buijzen, "Identifying Determinants of Young Children's Brand Awareness: Television, Parents, and Peers," *Journal of Applied Developmental Psychology* 26, no. 4 (2005): 456-468, doi: 10.1016/j.appdev.2005.04.004.

47. In the study, researchers showed the children logos of 12 brand name companies, including McDonald's, Nike, Heineken, Snuggle, and others. Children were asked to mention the name of the brand (brand recall) and to identify a product associated with that brand (brand recognition). On average, 2- to 3-year-olds recalled the name of about 1 of the 12 brands, but were able to associate nearly 8 of 12 products with the correct brand. In other words, 2-year-olds—yes, you read the age right—are able to identify that a McDonalds' product is associated with the golden arches! And 8-year-olds could do the same for 11.72 out of 12 products/brands on average.

48. Xiaomei Cai and Xiaoquan Zhao, "Click Here Kids! Online Advertising Practices on Children's Websites," *Journal of Children and Media* 4, no. 2 (2010): 135-154, doi: 10.1080/1748279100362910.

49. Amy Ustjanauskas, Jennifer Harris, and Marlene Schwartz, "Food and Beverage Advertising on Children's Web Sites," *Pediatric Obesity* 9, no. 5 (2013): 362-372, doi: 10.1111/j.2047-6310.2013.00185.x.

50. Victoria Rideout, Ulla Foehr, and Donald Roberts, *Generation M²: Media in the Lives of 8- to 18-year-olds* (Menlo Park, CA: Kaiser Family Foundation, 2010), 1-79, https://kaiserfamilyfoundation.files.wordpress.com/2013/01/8010.pdf.

51. Ibid.

52. Nicole Martins et al., "A Content Analysis of Female Body Imagery in Video Games," *Sex Roles* 61, no. 11-12 (2009): 824-836, doi: 10.1007/s11199-009-9682-9.

53. For each of these characters, the researchers measured their height, head width, chest width, waist width, and hip width. They also rated how visually realistic each game was in the level of detail displayed. They then compared the measurements of the characters to a nationally representative sample of 6,000 US citizens.

54. Martins et al., "A Content Analysis of Female Body Imagery in Video Games," 824-836.

55. Edward Downs and Stacy Smith, "Keeping Abreast of Hypersexuality: A Video Game Character Content Analysis," *Sex Roles* 62, no. 11-12 (2010): 721-733, doi: 10.1007/s11199-009-9637-1.

56. About 86% of the identifiable characters in 60 of the best-selling console games were male, 14% female. About 41% of female characters were shown wearing revealing clothing, compared to only 11% of male characters. In addition, 43% of female characters were depicted as partially or fully nude, compared to only 4% of male characters. The bodies of female characters were also much more likely to be depicted in an unrealistic way (25%) than the bodies of male characters (2%). Female characters were also more likely to have small waists (40%) compared to male characters (1%).

57. Downs and Smith, "Keeping Abreast of Hypersexuality: A Video Game Character Content Analysis," 721-733.

58. It was around this time that I distinctly recall asking my dad for $5 so I could go with my friends down to the arcade, a quaint little place called Wunderland. I loved how the light from the arcade screens was the only source of light in the building.

59. Claude Braun and Josette Giroux, "Arcade Video Games: Proxemic, Cognitive and Content Analyses," *Journal of Leisure Research* 21, no. 2 (1989): 92-105, www.researchgate.net/publication/232564888_Arcade_video_games_Proxemic_cognitive_and_content_analyses.

60. Tracy Dietz, "An Examination of Violence and Gender Role Portrayals in Video Games: Implications for Gender Socialization and Aggressive Behavior," *Sex Roles* 38, no. 5-6 (1998): 425-442, doi: 10.1023/A:1018709905920.

61. Stacy Smith, Ken Lachlan, and Ron Tamborini, "Popular Video Games: Quantifying the Presentation of Violence and Its Context," *Journal of Broadcasting and Electronic Media* 47, no. 1 (2003): 58-76, doi: 10.1207/s15506878jobem4701_4.

62. Karen Dill et al., "Violence, Sex, Race, and Age in Popular Video Games: A Content Analysis," in *Featuring Females: Feminist Analyses of Media*, eds. Ellen Cole and Jessica Daniel (Washington, DC: American Psychological Association, 2005), 115-130.

63. Amanda Lenhart, Kristen Purcell, Aaron Smith, and Kathryn Zickuhr, "Social Media and Young Adults," Pew Research Center, February 3, 2010, www.pewinternet.org/2010/02/03/social-media-and-young-adults/.

64. Common Sense Media, "Zero to Eight: Children's Media Use in America," (Washington D.C.: Common Sense Media, 2011).

65. David Finkelhor, Kimberly Mitchell, and Janis Wolak, *Online Victimization: A Report on the Nation's Youth* (Alexandria, VA: National Center for Missing and Exploited Children, 2000).

66. Cai and Zhao, "Click Here Kids! Online Advertising Practices on Children's Websites," 135-154.

67. Federal Trade Commission, *Protecting Children's Privacy Under COPPA: A Survey on Compliance* (Washington, DC: Federal Trade Commission, 2002).

68. Bianca Klettke, David Hallford, and David Mellor, "Sexting Prevalence and Correlates: A Systematic Literature Review," *Clinical Psychology Review* 34, no. 1 (2014): 44-53, doi: 10.1016/j.cpr.2013.10.007.

69. Victoria Rideout, *Zero to Eight: Children's Media Use in America 2013* (San Francisco, CA: Common Sense Media, 2013), 1-38.

70. Deborah Linebarger et al., "What Makes Preschool Educational Television Educational? A Content Analysis of Literacy, Language-Promoting, and Prosocial Preschool Programming," in *Media Exposure During Infancy and Early Childhood*, eds. Rachel Barr and Deborah Linebarger (Switzerland: Springer, 2017), 97-133.

# 3 Media Effects
## The Influence of Media on Children

So far, we've talked about the amount and types of media content to which our children are exposed. But what does this exposure mean for our kids? Does it affect them in any way? The answer is, of course, yes.

My younger brother and I are less than two years apart, but growing up he was always just as tall as me. People used to ask us if we were twins, and I got so tired of explaining that I was almost two years older. We did everything together. We used to ride our bikes on the street in front of our home and pretend we were Ponch and Jon from *CHIPS*. I was Jon. He was Ponch. We also used to practice climbing into our family car through the windows when we played Dukes of Hazzard. I was Bo. He was Luke. We played in the backyard so much that we wore the grass down to the dirt in several places. We made a pretty good team. Until we watched *Karate Kid*.

When I was young, I wanted to be Daniel LaRusso. You remember Daniel. Karate Kid. Mr. Miyagi. Johnny. And Ali, with an "i." After Daniel wins the tournament at the end of the show, my brother and I would inevitably start practicing karate on each other. We perfected the crane move that Daniel used to beat Johnny. We got so good at karate (or so we thought), that one time I got mad at him for spilling grape juice on my favorite blanket and punched him as hard as I could. I felt horrible about what I did, so I begged him to hit me back. While I can't remember if he hit me back or not, this is the first instance I can recall of being directly influenced by media exposure. My behavior changed both temporarily (practicing our karate moves on each other), and long-term (thinking that fighting was the right way to solve a problem).

On the flip side, I also remember being positively affected by watching something on TV. Growing up, I loved basketball. I still do. These days, I hobble around the court playing what is most appropriately called "old man ball." When I was in high school, I used to bring my basketball to bed with me. I'd wake up well before the sun came up many mornings just to go out in the backyard and dribble my ball. I watched as much basketball on TV as I could and fell in love with the NCAA men's basketball tournament. I'm trying to pass that love on to my kids (every year we each complete a bracket of our own). My first memory of NCAA basketball occurred in 1987. Those were the days of Dean Smith, Bobby Knight, and Tark the Shark chewing on his towel. That year, Indiana and Syracuse played each other in the national championship game. Keith Smart, a player on Indiana, scored the game-winning basket to lift Indiana over Syracuse for the national championship. It was a thing of beauty. A smooth jumper on the left baseline. After the last game of each NCAA tournament, the TV producers put together a montage of video clips from the tournament and set it to Luther Vandross singing "One Shining Moment." I still get chills when I watch it. After watching the game that day in 1987, and after hearing the song for the first time, I decided right then and there that I'd do whatever it took to play in the NCAA tournament myself. Short-term, I spent the next several days outside with a ball in my hands, dribbling and shooting. Long-term, I tried really hard to make myself into a player worthy of being recruited by college scouts. I tried hard, I really did. But I was too small, too slow, and just not good enough to get a sniff. I attribute my efforts, at least in part, to watching Keith Smart and hearing the smooth voice of Luther Vandross singing the anthem of American basketball.

Media exposure has an effect. Statistically speaking, research shows that the effect of media exposure is generally "small" to "moderate." But small statistics can change big things. A few votes here and a few votes there can change an entire election. Many games are won by the slimmest of margins. And just one more drink can send a person over the top, can't it? That's the type of small to moderate effect we're talking about. A good way to think about media effects is to describe them as "meaningful." We often don't know exactly how much of an attitude or behavior can be directly attributed to something we saw in the media, but we do know that watching something in the media can have a meaningful effect on us. Media exposure may be the factor that changes things just enough for children. When we talk of the media's effect on kids, we generally talk about the media's effect on their "well-being." Parents, researchers, and educators are all interested in how media exposure can both positively and negatively influence children's well-being. To be sure, there is a lot tied up in the term *well-being*. But instead of describing all the potential meanings of the term, let's briefly review what the research says about each of the types of content we talked about in the previous chapter. There is, of course, not enough room here to talk about all the research, but this is an honest attempt to summarize the thousands of studies about these topics. So, we'll start where we always start: the Big 4.

## Violence

With every widely publicized act of senseless violence in America, such as a mass shooting or terrorist bombing, comes a wave of criticism of the media. It's funny; the media blame the media for contributing to the delusions that cause people to commit these horrific crimes against innocent people. So, is the media to blame?

When we talk about the effect of media violence, we are actually talking about a bunch of things. Generally, people want to know if exposure to media violence increases children's aggression. One way to measure this is to simply ask young people how often they use violent media content (such as playing violent video games or watching certain shows), and then ask them questions that measure their aggression. Not surprisingly, several such studies doing just this have found a correlation between exposure to violent media and aggression. Correlation, however, does not necessarily mean that one causes the other—it is perfectly possible in studies such as this that children who are already predisposed to behave aggressively tend to gravitate toward violent media content more often. In fact, that is an entirely plausible explanation. So, survey research only gets us so far. Experiments, on the other hand, can get at causation. In one of the first experiments involving violent video game effects, 210 college students came to a laboratory and played either a violent or nonviolent video game for half an hour under the guise that researchers wanted to learn about the development of motor skills used in activities like video games.[1] Throughout the session, participants took breaks and answered several survey questions. About a week later, the same participants came back to the lab and played the video game again. This time, however, after playing the game for 15 minutes, they each participated in a competitive reaction time task against an opponent. The goal of the task was to push a button faster than the opponent. The winner of the task then sent a noise blast to the loser at a volume supposedly set by the winner, when in reality the volume was actually set by a computer. This means that if the participant won, they could presumably choose the intensity and duration of the noise blast for their opponent. This is an often-used measure of aggressive behavior. Not surprisingly, those who played the violent video game delivered longer noise blasts to their opponents. They also had more aggressive thoughts, measured as how quickly they read violent words (such as "murder") compared to similar-length nonviolent words (such as "report") when they appeared on a computer screen. Although we could argue that in real life we don't display aggression by sending long and loud noise blasts (except, maybe, by honking the horn at someone who cuts us off while driving), this study provided some of the first evidence that video games have a direct effect on aggressive thoughts and behaviors.

A study involving 52 elementary school children showed similar results when children watched television violence.[2] Half of the children were assigned to watch a 22-minute episode of *Mighty Morphin Power Rangers* that contained about 140 acts of aggression, while the other half did not view the program. In subsequent regular classroom play, children in the *Power Rangers* condition committed 7 acts of aggression for every 1 act of aggression by those in the control condition.[3]

Dr. Brad Bushman was a member of the communications faculty when I was a graduate student at The Ohio State University. Dr. Bushman is perhaps the world's preeminent authority on media violence and its effects. And he's a good guy, to boot. He has testified before the US Congress about youth violence, and in 2014, he received the Distinguished Lifetime Contribution to Media Psychology and Technology from the American Psychological Association. He and his colleague, L. Rowell Huesmann, conducted what's called a meta-analysis of the media violence research literature.[4] A meta-analysis is a fancy way of saying that they gathered all the relevant published research about media violence and used some advanced statistics to test the overall effect of exposure to media violence. Their meta-analysis included hundreds of studies with tens of thousands of children and adult participants. The results showed that exposure to violence in the media, such as in TV, movies, video games, music, and comic books, is related to increased aggressive behavior, decreased helpful behavior, increased aggressive thoughts, increased angry feelings, and heightened levels of physiological arousal (such as heart rate and blood pressure). In their opinion, and mine, the case is clear and closed. Exposure to media violence is one of the causes of children's aggression.

Please note that I said "one of the causes." It is by no means the only cause, and by and large the effect size is what we'd call small to moderate. This means that there are many other factors that go into children's aggressive thoughts and behaviors. Maybe some kids are predisposed for aggression. Some kids might learn from adult examples that aggression is an effective way to solve problems. How tired kids are, how hungry they are, their history of being a victim of abuse, and a host of other things may also predict children's aggression. Media exposure is one of those things. It's probably a combination of many things that causes aggression.

Research on the effects of television can be traced back to two early studies, one in England in 1958, and one in North America in 1961. That time period was unique in the history of the world. This was the time when television was just starting to become mainstream. Some people had TV, but many still did not. Kind of like Netflix today—despite what it seems, some people still don't use Netflix (including me). Both of these early studies are unique in that they were able to compare children who had televisions in their home to children who did not have televisions in their home. The 1958 British study found that children with a TV in their home learned the following themes from watching TV: life is difficult, marriages are frequently unhappy, parent-child relationships are frequently strained, life events seldom bring happiness, and violence is inevitable, even for "good" people.[5] Children with TVs were also more prone to nightmares and insomnia and were disturbed by depictions of daggers, sharp instruments, guns, and swords. Violence on TV led to aggression for emotionally disturbed children. And those with a TV in their home experienced tiredness and a lack of concentration at school. The 1961 North American study involved five communities in the US and two in Canada.[6] Again, kids where TV was available exhibited more fear and were less able to detach TV from reality. They also had what the authors called a disproportionate view of society, meaning they expected to find a greater proportion of "sexy" women, more violent acts, more deadbeat dads, more get-rich-quick careers, and more corrupt law enforcement officials than actually appear in the real world. To support these findings, some statistics show that between 1960 (about when television became mainstream in American homes) and 1991, the population of America grew by 40% but the violent crime rate grew by 500%.[7] TV, it seems, may be one of the factors that contributes to violence in America.

Despite the overwhelming evidence that exposure to violent media content causes aggression, there are those in our society that still resist the idea that they or anybody else can be influenced by media exposure. This is disturbing on many levels. First, it goes against decades of scientific research showing otherwise, and second, it directly contradicts basic common sense. If I ate ten donuts a day for a year, I would get fat. If all I knew about women was what I learned while viewing pornography, my view of women would be highly distorted. And if I viewed ten thousand murders and other physical assaults on TV every year (which statistics show may be the case), it is simply reasonable that my thoughts and behaviors would be altered in some way. I could go study by study to show the overwhelming evidence for the link between violent media exposure and children's aggression, but I think you get the point.

## Sexual Content

As mentioned previously, the media has arguably become our children's most common sex educator. Personally, I think this is true. Bless my parents, but I grew up in a home where sex was a bad word, or at least I perceived it that way. I don't recall ever having the sex talk with my parents. Maybe we had the talk and I've simply blocked it from memory. Sex education in my little hometown was taught in seventh grade. I remember sitting in rickety chairs in an old, dark gymnasium having a sex ed class taught by our gym teacher. As many seventh grade boys in the same situation, I found my mind wandering and wishing I was anywhere but there, and then the teacher called my name. She had just asked me a question. I asked her to repeat it: "Why can't people get STDs from doorknobs and toilet seats?" she asked. I had no idea, but I was quick enough on my feet to answer, "Because people don't have sex with doorknobs and toilet seats." That got a good laugh out of my friends, and my teacher, but it was at that moment I realized that I was clueless when it came to sex. And because my parents were pretty strict about what we could watch on TV, I learned about sex in conversations with friends. I remember hearing my friends use terms such as "jacking off," "blow job," and "69." I had no idea what these terms meant, and I was sure everybody else did. I had no idea where my friends learned these things—all I knew is that I was largely uneducated when it came to sex. So, I did my best to decipher the meaning of such sex-related lingo from context cues in these conversations. You can imagine how well that went. This is all to say that the typical American child may not be learning about sex from responsible adults, either at home or at school. And most parents don't limit media exposure like mine did, so the only way some kids these days learn about sex is from the media, or from their friends who share what they learn from media.

Well, what is it then that children today are learning about sex from the media, and what effect do these messages have? To be short in writing, today's youth learn from media exposure that sex is "a casual pastime, a romp in the hay, with little or no consequences."[8] And the consequences are what you might think. For example, a study involving more than 1,000 youth ages 12–16 in Southern California[9] found that kids who watched more sexual content on cable TV programming were more likely to report having participated in sexual intercourse and oral sex.[10] These same kids were also more likely to report greater intentions to have oral sex and sexual intercourse in the future. It should be noted that the same pattern of results did not emerge for exposure to sexual content on broadcast television, only on cable TV, for whatever reason. Maybe sexual content as portrayed on cable TV is different, or more explicit, than sexual content portrayed on broadcast TV due to content rules for broadcast TV providers. In addition, the kids who watched more sexual content on cable TV also did not see that having sex would have as many negative consequences as youth who watched relatively less sexual content. And finally, kids who watched more sexual content on either broadcast or cable TV were less likely to believe that participating in sexual activities would result in health problems.

In addition to the effect of sexual media exposure on sexual behaviors, sexual media exposure can change the way children think. In one study involving youth ages 14–18 in New York, researchers asked participants about how often they see several forms of sexual content on television.[11] The study found that the more sexy prime-time TV participants watched, the more strongly they supported recreational sex. And the more they watched television because they felt like TV was a good companion, the more they approved of recreational sex, the more they thought that men are driven by sex, and the more they thought of women as sex objects (for example, thinking that the best way for a girl to attract a guy is to use her body and looks).

Using their body and looks to attract a guy may be the last thing I want my daughters to do. While I think my daughters are beautiful, their appearance is at the bottom of a long list of attributes that makes them that way. But because sexual content in the media seems to be inseparably connected with how people view women, society tends to place more value on females' appearance than on their competence-based attributes. I discuss this and other issues related to the portrayal of women and girls in the media in some detail in the Appendix at the end of the book.

We could spend an entire book reviewing the research on the effects of sexual television, and on the sexualization of girls in the media—and there are some books that do just that—but I'll simply share a list of the effects of exposure to sexual media compiled by scholars in my field:[12]

- The belief that casual sex, without any sort of relational commitment, is acceptable.
- The attitude that obtaining pleasure is more important than establishing a relationship with one's sex partner.
- The belief that men are driven by sex.
- The belief that women are sex objects.

- The belief that media can be sexually arousing.
- The reality that kids start having sex at a younger age.
- Kids seeking out new sexual experiences.
- Boys' sexual harassment of girls.
- Increased teen pregnancy rates.
- Higher rates of contracting sexually transmitted diseases.
- More sexual partners.
- Greater likelihood of having unprotected sex with a stranger.

Is this enough to at least make your brow wrinkle a little? While the results are not totally conclusive or consistent across studies, the fact that any study found these relationships is cause enough for parental concern. If these results are true, then we should be concerned about both visual and nonvisual media. In other words, even the music our kids listen to can have an effect. For example, country music is often considered the most benign, or innocent, of all music genres. In 2014, a new female country duo named Maddie & Tae released a song called "Girl in a Country Song." The song suggests that country music has changed since the "good ol' days." Today, the song says, girls are lucky if they get to wear something besides a bikini top and painted-on jeans. They say that country music makes women feel like they have to climb into the cab of some guy's truck and shut up, shake their moneymaker or sugar shaker (which, apparently, are references to a woman's backside), and have long tan legs. In essence, whether the singers meant to or not, the song is a critique of the current "good-old-boy" country culture that views women as sex objects. As a follow-up to the song, I worked with Rebecca Densley, a great researcher who focuses on what parents can do about sexual media content, to see if what the song says is true. We analyzed the lyrics of 750 country songs between 1990 and 2014 and found that in the 2010s, women are significantly more objectified than they were in songs in the 1990s and 2000s.[13] When women are sung about in these more recent song lyrics, it is more often about their physical appearance or wearing of tight or revealing clothing than in past decades. In other words, even country music is becoming more objectifying of women. It remains to be seen what the effects of this are, but based on past research, we can only imagine.

For example, let's look at the long-standing issue of how women's perceptions of their own bodies are negatively affected by sexual media content. We've all likely heard criticisms of the typical thin body shapes of animated Disney princesses. But research shows that the appearance of real-life "Disney Girls" also has a striking impact on how tween girls view themselves. If your daughters are like mine, they know who Selena Gomez, Miley Cyrus (the pre-twerking Miley), Taylor Swift, and Demi Lovato are. It turns out that tween girls don't just know who these girls are, but they get their lessons on what it means to be beautiful from them. In one study,[14] researchers interviewed girls ages 9–11 and had them create photo collages of women in the media. Here's what researchers found about tween girls' perceptions of the "ideal" body:

- The ideal body is not too heavy and not too thin. Somewhere around a size seven.
- Girls smaller than that want to be heavier and girls bigger than that want to be thinner.
- Certain practices are required to be pretty, such as wearing matching clothes, using makeup, eating and exercising in moderation, and having nicely brushed hair and clear skin.
- It requires money to be pretty. "Ugly" girls look the way they do because they lack the money it takes to be "pretty."

And guess who tween girls said were the ideals of beauty to which they aspired—that's right, Selena Gomez, Miley Cyrus, Demi Lovato, and Taylor Swift.[15] It's clear then—and it's no surprise—that there is social pressure to look a certain way, even if it's not the extremely thin, big-busted woman we hear about the most as the "ideal" shape for a woman. The study also found that tween girls have certain ideas of what looking a certain way would do for them socially. They said that if they looked like the real-life "Disney Girls," they would,

- Have lots of money.
- Be treated differently.
- Have lots of friends.
- Be more popular, and thus, happier.
- Get more attention from boys.
- Not get picked on as much.

## Pornography

Our discussion about sexual media content would not be complete without a discussion about pornography. While there is some research—albeit very little—that suggests that pornography can have some positive sexual effects for adults, an overwhelming majority of the research concludes that pornography has both direct and indirect *negative* effects on those who view it and on their loved ones.

For example, in one study I conducted with other researchers, we describe research showing that females who view pornography "are more likely to accept rape myths and sexual violence against women, be accepting of premarital and extramarital sex, place less value on marriage and monogamy, desire to have children less, accept male dominance and female submission, and overestimate certain sexual behaviors."[16] That's quite a list, but that only includes research related to females' use of pornography themselves.

Girls, especially, are also affected by their relational partner's pornography use, often in the form of reduced self-esteem, insecurity about their bodies, feelings of worthlessness and unattractiveness, feelings of inadequacy, of being cheating on, degraded, and misunderstood. The list goes on. For males, pornography exposure (and not just at the level of addiction) is related to lower sexual and relational satisfaction,[17] "less progressive gender role attitudes," "more permissive sexual norms," "perpetration of sexual harassment," participation in oral sex and sexual intercourse,[18] attitudes in support of violence against women,[19] lower sexual self-esteem,[20] more recreational attitudes toward sex,[21] and the notion of women as sex objects.[22] In addition, the more young people view pornography, the more they seek out new and novel pornographic material in order to reach the same level of enjoyment.[23]

What's more, most of these findings that I've just reported were from studies involving adolescents or college students. Very little research has explored effects of children's use of pornography. But, I should note here again that absolutely no reputable research suggests that viewing pornography is in any way good for children. None. Zip. Zero. I won't even allow an argument about that fact. In terms of the media maze, then, evidence suggests that viewing pornography is a dead end for both adults and children.

The portrayal of sex, especially as it relates to the media's portrayal of women in sexy and objectifying ways, has the effects that you imagined it would. Boys and girls of all ages are indeed affected by sexual media content.

## Substance Use

We've already discussed the content of alcohol commercials—fun, sexy, healthy, young people who spend their weekends drinking, with no consequences. And as you might guess, yes, research shows a correlation between exposure to alcohol in the media and subsequent consumption of alcohol. One of the classic studies[24] in this line of research was conducted in the UK and involved nearly 1,000 teenagers ages 12–16 who were classified as either drinkers or nondrinkers at the beginning of the study.[25] The study found that among kids who were classified as nondrinkers at the beginning of the two-year study, 47% of them had started drinking by the time they finished the study. What's more, statistical analyses found that a significant predictor of their uptake of drinking alcohol was their awareness of and interest in alcohol marketing, even when taking into account a host of other variables. Similar results have been found in many other studies and have been replicated in both Europe and the United States. One study even found that exposure to alcohol advertisements in the seventh grade was related to youths' alcohol use in the tenth grade; the study concluded that younger adolescents (those in the seventh grade) seem to be especially susceptible to the persuasive way that alcohol is packaged in advertisements.[26]

To say it lightly, drinking alcohol is an enormous problem among college students in the United States. The National Institute on Alcohol Abuse and Alcoholism (NIAAA) stated that "college drinking is extremely widespread" since about 4 out of 5 college students drink alcohol.[27] They further stated that "virtually all college students experience the effects of college drinking—whether they drink or not." The NIAAA website also cites the following statistics:

- Nearly 2,000 college students die each year from alcohol-related unintentional injuries.
- Nearly 700,000 college students are assaulted each year by another student who had been drinking.
- Nearly 100,000 college students are the victim of alcohol-related sexual assault or date rape.
- 1.2–1.5% of college students said they have tried to commit suicide within the past year due to drinking or using drugs.

Because these statistics are pretty frightening, researchers have tried to pinpoint all the factors that contribute to college students' alcohol consumption. Interestingly, this research shows that light and moderate drinkers increase their alcohol consumption to levels above what they would otherwise consume simply because they overestimate the amount of alcohol that their peers consume.[28] Turns out there are dozens of studies showing that college students consistently overestimate how much their peers drink. And because we have a tendency to engage in behaviors that we believe other people who are like us also do, drinking levels in college are higher than they would be if college students had an accurate perception of the typical amount of drinking that takes place. We see this because campaigns designed to inform students about the real prevalence of drinking among college students have actually helped reduce drinking among college students.[29] The question then becomes, where do college students get the idea that their peers are drinking much more than they actually are? You guessed it—from the media (at least in part). Media exposure is also related to perceptions about the prevalence of tobacco use.[30] It is important to note here that although the studies I've referred to so far generally talk about alcohol use in association with television exposure, teens' use of social networking sites is also related to increased use of alcohol, marijuana, and tobacco.[31]

That brings us to a brief discussion about the effects of media exposure on tobacco use. Not surprisingly, dozens of studies involving nearly 400,000 youth participants reveal a definitive connection between exposure to tobacco marketing and youths' consumption of tobacco products.[32] I won't get into the details of individual studies here, but due to the overwhelming amount of research that corroborates the link between tobacco in the media and smoking, the National Cancer Institute issued the following statement: "Media communications play a key role in shaping tobacco-related knowledge, opinions, attitudes, and behaviors among individuals and within communities . . . the total weight of evidence— from multiple types of studies, conducted by investigators from different disciplines, and using data from many countries—demonstrates a causal relationship between tobacco advertising and promotion and increased tobacco use."[33] And just to be sure you read that right, note that the word used is "causal," not "casual." There's a big difference.

Because of the connection between media images of smoking, one study estimated that portrayals of smoking in movies accounts for the initiation of smoking of nearly 400,000 teenagers annually.[34] When extrapolated out to revenue for the US tobacco industry, estimates suggest that portrayals of smoking in movies alone translates into about $4.1 billion in revenue, and $894 million in profits, to American tobacco companies.[35]

## Advertising

Not too long ago, my family was sitting in front of the TV after a long day of work and school. Often in the evenings we spend some time just decompressing in front of the TV to a show that we all enjoy. Some of our favorites are *American Ninja Warrior*, the kids' version of one of those top chef shows, reruns of *The Middle* and *Last Man Standing*, and other reality competition shows like *America's Got Talent*. On this particular night, I think we were watching *The Voice*. It went to a commercial, and on came an advertisement about a moisturizing cream. At the end of the commercial our then six-year-old turned to me and said, "Dad, we need to have moist skin like that."

Talk about effective advertising.

When it comes to advertising, I'm especially sensitive to ads directed toward women and girls. Having a wife and four daughters will do that to a man. I've concluded that, in a way, all media content is an advertisement of some sort since we develop our tastes, our wants, our desires, and what we think is cool and popular based on what we see in the media. And the media tells us that to look a certain way often involves spending money. Research suggests that this message seems to be creeping down to, and affecting, even young girls. As if adolescence isn't hard enough already, research shows that girls as young as six prefer provocative clothing and feel dissatisfied with their bodies. Researchers in Australia[36] asked three hundred girls ages six to nine how often they watch several popular television shows or look at popular magazines and asked them questions about their clothing and body size preferences and about boys' clothing preferences for girls.[37] Results showed that the more girls watched "sexualized" TV (the "sexiness" of the shows was rated by independent coders), the more they thought that boys would like more provocative clothing. In addition, the more they looked at sexualized magazines, the more they preferred provocative clothing for themselves. While exposure to sexualized media was not directly related to being less satisfied with their body, girls who preferred sexier clothing for themselves and who thought sexy clothing is popular with other girls tended to be less satisfied with their bodies.

Advertisers spend billions trying to create these attitudes with the hope that they can convince girls to go out and buy "sexy" clothing in order to impress boys. To buy pills, creams, and lotions that help them feel thinner and prettier. The traditional American media system is owned by only a handful of corporations, and our daughters are learning from them what it means to be a girl. Did you catch that? Corporations, whose sole purpose is to capture as much wealth as possible, are inundating our daughters with messages about their value, and those values often result in girls spending money on "stuff" to help them feel better about themselves because of the media content that these corporations put on air in the first place! Talk about a vicious cycle! As Dr. Juliet B. Schor, professor of sociology at Boston College, said, "Children's social worlds are increasingly constructed around consuming, as brands and products have come to determine who is 'in' or 'out,' who is hot or not, who deserves to have friends or social status."[38]

Research paints a very consistent picture that shows exposure to advertising has several clear effects on children. One area of the most interest when it comes to children and advertising is advertising's effect on children's food intake—both the amount and type of food they consume. Research in this area has consistently concluded that food advertising on television increases the amount of food children eat. For example, in one study, some children saw a food commercial while watching a cartoon, while other children saw a nonfood commercial during the cartoon.[39] A snack was made available to participants during the experiment. Children who saw the food commercial during the cartoon ate an astounding 45% more of the snack than children who saw the nonfood advertisement. In 2010, The World Health Organization issued a report after reviewing the research on the relationship between advertising and children's food consumption and concluded that "television advertising influences children's food preferences, purchase requests and consumption patterns."[40] Based on their review of the evidence, they felt strongly enough about the connection between advertising and children's obesity that they issued a call for policy that would help reduce the exposure of children to "marketing of foods high in saturated fats, trans-fatty acids, free sugars, and salt."[41]

Advertising also creates a desire for other products. One of the most interesting studies I've seen about children and advertising was conducted by two researchers in the Netherlands—Dr. Moniek Buijzen and Dr. Patti Valkenburg.[42] They asked 250 children ages 7–12 to make a list of what they wanted for Christmas and compared these wish lists with the advertisements on the TV networks that the kids watched.[43] Results showed that the amount of time children spent watching one of the TV networks was related to the number of toys listed by children on their Christmas lists that were consistent with the brands on the television commercials. More than half of the children in the study included at least one brand that had been advertised on the networks on their Christmas wish list. In other words, the brands that children requested on their Christmas lists were consistent with the brands found in the advertising to which they were exposed.

Including popular media figures in an advertisement seems to make products more desirable for children. For example, one study involving 216 kids ages 4–6 found that children wanted to buy fruit packaged with a picture of Dora (from *Dora the Explorer)* or SpongeBob just as much as they wanted to buy candy.[44] You might remember seeing similar character endorsements as a kid—Bart Simpson loved Butterfinger bars, Tony the Tiger liked Frosted Flakes, and McDonald's Happy Meals always seemed to contain a toy coinciding with a recently released movie. Even now, I find myself gravitating toward basketball shoes with the Air Jordan logo on them. I don't know why. I suppose I've become brand loyal. That's exactly what advertising does—it makes us brand loyal, and advertisers know that if they can create brand loyalty among kids, they'll grow up as loyal, repeat customers of common consumer products.

Advertising has also been found to be related to children's materialism, the "idea that money and possessions are important and that certain qualities such as beauty and success can be obtained from having material property."[45] Advertising also creates conflict between parents and children, as parents often feel nagged by their children to buy certain products.[46] I can't count the number of times I've been walking through the grocery store when I've heard parents tell their children to stop asking them to buy things for them. My kids are no exception. We live in a world filled to the brim and overflowing with advertising. Of course advertising has an effect.

## Video Games

I never had a video game console growing up. If I wanted to play video games, I had to go to a friend's house or my cousin's house. I was always extremely jealous of my cousin, especially when he used a secret code to bypass many levels to be able to reach the top where he could fight Mike Tyson in *Mike Tyson's Punch-Out!!* I love my cousin, but he never did share the code with me. The scoundrel. The first gun I ever held was the Duck Hunt gun. And I learned that as long as Bo Jackson was on my TecmoBowl team, I could usually win. Back then, I never thought about the effects of video games. As a dad, I think about it quite a bit. My kids don't have a video game console. They play games on the tablet every now and then, but we really try to keep video games to a minimum. It's a choice we've made as a family. I just think there are so many other productive things that could be done with time besides playing video games. Other families might find that they draw closer together by playing video games with each other. Some parents think some games encourage creativity and cooperation. And the thing is, we're all probably right. So that you can make an informed decision in your family, let's now talk about some of the research related to the effects of playing video games.

Video games are of concern to some parents because they can contain content that we've already talked about, such as violence and sex. Not surprisingly, much of the research involving video games has focused on their violent content. Violence in video games, however, is different than violence on TV and in the movies. Video games provide a different experience—in many cases, players aren't watching others perpetrate violence—they are the ones perpetrating the simulated violence. Research overwhelmingly shows that playing violent video games is related to aggressive behaviors, thoughts, and emotions. In addition, playing violent video games is related to a decrease in prosocial behaviors.

When video game studies are conducted, it's obviously not ethical to see if video game playing makes people hit, punch, or otherwise physically harm other research participants. Could you imagine you or your children participating in a study like that? Instead, many studies involving violent video games measure aggressive behavior by looking at participants' engagement in activities that they *think* are actually happening, such as giving another person an electric shock or a loud blast of noise, as we've already discussed. And because thoughts and feelings often precede behaviors, many studies also measure the effect of video game playing on aggressive thoughts and feelings. So, when we talk about video game research, we have to combine all these different measures of aggression in order to determine if playing video games has an overall effect on children's aggression. Do you remember the term we used before, *meta-analysis*? To reiterate, a meta-analysis looks at all the studies on a given topic and uses certain statistical tests to summarize what the combined research says. Researchers conducted a meta-analysis of video game research and found that playing video games is significantly and statistically related to increases in aggressive behaviors, thoughts, and feelings, as well as decreases in empathy and prosocial behaviors.[47]

Of course, there are video games that are not violent, or if they are violent, they require cooperation and helping in some way. One study found that the more kids play prosocial video games, the more they behave in prosocial ways.[48] By prosocial, we mean doing things such as helping and sharing, or the opposite of antisocial behaviors such as aggressive acts. That's all fine and dandy, but as we know, simply because they are related doesn't mean one causes the other. It could be that kids who often behave in prosocial ways simply tend to play more prosocial games. That is a logical conclusion as well. For example, kids (5th graders) reported their video game use and their prosocial behaviors once (time 1) and then again 3–4 months later (time 2). They found that prosocial game playing at time 1 predicted prosocial behavior at time 2—evidence of an effect of playing prosocial games on kids' prosocial behavior. In addition, prosocial behavior at time 1 also predicted prosocial game playing at time 2, meaning that kids who are more prosocial tended to seek out prosocial game playing. In other words, the authors argue, these findings suggest an "upward spiral" where playing prosocial games leads to prosocial behavior, which leads to more prosocial gaming, and so on.

What about video games that are violent but that require teamwork and other forms of cooperation? A couple of friends and colleagues of mine, Dr. Dave Ewoldsen and Dr. John Velez, were among a group of researchers that asked that very question in a study involving 119 college students, mainly males.[49] They invited participants to come into a lab to play *Halo 2* on an Xbox 360. *Halo 2*, as you may know, is a violent "first person shooter" game where the object of the game is basically to kill humans and aliens. The player plays from the perspective of the person pulling the trigger. In the study, some people played in competition with others, while some people had to work together with others. After playing, subjects then participated in a game where they could either work together with someone or they could work alone toward a goal. The study found that people who played the game cooperatively with another person exhibited higher levels of cooperative behavior in the follow-up game than those who played the game competitively against others.

So, what does this mean? First, this means that playing video games isn't inherently bad. Just like watching TV isn't inherently bad. What seems to be most important is the content of the video games. And that makes perfect sense based on what we know about other media effects, doesn't it? The more we fill our minds with violent images, the more our thoughts, feelings, and behaviors will tend to mirror those images. Similarly, if we fill our minds with images of helping, sharing, and cooperation, the more our thoughts, feelings, and behaviors will tend to mirror those images. And second, this means that the context of video game playing makes a difference, in addition to the game's content. Playing with others to achieve a common goal appears to increase prosocial behavior. However, this doesn't mean that simply playing violent video games with a teammate completely negates any effect of the violence on players' aggression. I suppose, then, that decisions need to be made about whether or not the good effects of playing video games outweigh the bad effects.

**Internet/Social Media**

My wife and I met when we were sixteen years old. We happened to be at the same conference for high school journalists in Washington, DC. We also happened to live on opposite sides of the country. Today, that wouldn't have been a problem with video chatting, e-mail, texting, and all the other ways we can communicate. But way back in the ancient 1990s, all we had was the phone and snail mail. Back when we had to pay for long-distance calls (gasp!), Sunday nights after seven were the cheapest time of the week to make long distance calls. So, nearly every Sunday night, my future wife and I could each be found sprawled out on our respective floors, talking to each other on the phone. We also wrote a lot of letters to each other. Those were simple times.

Our children are growing up in a completely different world, where communication with anybody, anywhere in the world is near instantaneous. Oh, how I would have loved to see my future wife's face on a video chat all those Sunday nights long ago. Communication technologies today are amazing, and I'm jealous of my kids that they get to grow up in this day and age. We could spend time talking about all the good things that our children experience due to the Internet and social media, but the purpose of this book is largely to give parents tools to deal with aspects of media they are concerned about. I could spend an entire book talking about the potentially negative effects of using the Internet and social media, but I'll feature just a few so you get an idea of what the research says.

To what risks are kids more susceptible as a result of frequent Internet use? The results are all over place. Children who frequently use the Internet, especially at the level of Internet addiction (as measured by something called the Young Internet Addiction Test), are more likely to exhibit symptoms of depression.[50] Time spent on Facebook and other social networking sites is also related to symptoms of depression.[51] When we talk of Internet use and mental health, it should be noted that the editor of the American Journal of Psychiatry and other researchers have argued that Internet Addiction Disorder should be included in the DSM-5. The DSM is the Diagnostic and Statistical Manual of Mental Disorders and is the bible for mental health professionals for diagnosing mental health disorders. Those who use the Internet at excessive levels risk developing Internet Addiction Disorder—these people "share behavioral similarities with patients struggling with substance abuse, exhibiting psychological triggers, cravings, and addiction-seeking behaviors."[52] But aside from using the Internet at addiction levels, children's Internet use (when they frequently spend time online) is related to eye problems, headaches, not eating, tiredness, aggression, and sleeping problems—some of these problems occurred after only spending thirty minutes with technology![53]

Kids who spend time online are also at risk of experiencing online bullying and harassment. This is a problem because those who experience online harassment also experience greater psychological distress, symptoms of depressive, suicidal thoughts, and academic disengagement and delinquency.[54] Time spent using social networking sites is related to seeing sexual images on any websites, being bullied online, meeting new online contacts offline, receiving sexual messages, and seeing negative user-generated content (such as sites talking about self-harm, anorexia, and taking drugs).[55] Access to and nighttime use of electronic entertainment and communication devices, such as video games, computers, and smart phones—all of which are in some way related to spending time online—is related to "shortened sleep duration, excess body weight, poorer diet quality, and lower levels of physical activity."[56] Children who use the Internet more often are at risk for encountering unwanted sexual materials, unwanted sexual solicitations, and other forms of harassment.[57]

My 20th high school reunion was in 2016. Because I now live so far away from where I grew up, I could not attend, but I thought quite a bit about my high school days in the months leading up the 20th reunion. It made me feel old, of course. But I also realized that I don't look at my high school years very fondly, and I think it might be because I was the victim of bullying. Some of my classmates may be surprised to know that because of my religious affiliation, I was spit on during my high school years. I was called "stupid 'enter religious epithet here.'" Kids pulled pranks on me, and I was deliberately bumped into while walking down the hall. Until my senior year, I'll admit, going to school made me feel uneasy, and I became pretty good at avoiding certain people. Now, know that I'm over it. I'm secure in who I am, and I feel pity—not anger—toward those who bullied me. Back then, I didn't know it was bullying, but as a parent, it's very clear that bullying is exactly what it was. I don't share this to make you feel sorry for me. What I feel now is a need to protect my kids from experiencing what I experienced. But here's the difficult part about bullying these days. When I was in high school, we didn't have the Internet. Bullying was solely "traditional" back then. And just as kids are vulnerable to being exposed to a host of things online that were just not available when I was a kid, they are also more likely to be exposed to cyberbullying.

No parent wants their child to be involved in cyberbullying, either as the victim or the perpetrator. Though there are many factors that go into whether or not one is bullied or is a bully, research shows that the use of the Internet in certain ways makes kids more vulnerable to being the victim and/or the perpetrator of cyberbullying. For example, one study looked at 81 different studies related to cyberbullying—a total of nearly 100,000 participants. The study found that a common attribute of those who are victims of cyberbullying, and also of those who are the perpetrators of cyberbullying, is "risky information and communications technology use."[58] Or in other words, risky Internet use. Risky Internet use comes in several forms, including sharing personal information or photos of oneself online or becoming friends with someone who one has met only online. Such risky Internet use becomes problematic, according to the research, because people are more likely to say and do things online that they would not in a face-to-face setting, including saying and doing aggressive things. Another predictor of being the victim of cyberbullying is how much someone is bullied in the "traditional" sense, such as at school or in other social situations. Likewise, someone is more likely to become a cyberbully if they are a "traditional" bully.

Please know that I firmly believe that bullying is never, ever the victim's fault. Ever. But this research suggests that there are things we can teach our kids that could help them avoid bullies. This research suggests that children need to learn—preferably from parents—what types of online behaviors are safe and which are dangerous. Kids should never share personal information online. Kids should not become friends with strangers that they only know in an online setting. Kids should never agree to meet someone in person that they only know online. And as much as possible, parents should do whatever is necessary to determine if their child is either a victim or perpetrator of bullying in both traditional and online settings. StopBullying.gov is a good site that outlines signs that a child is being bullied, or bullying others, that parents should be aware of. The bottom line, then, appears to be consistent and effective parent-child communication about the Internet and vigilant monitoring of children's emotional states.

I'm no expert at bullying or cyberbullying. And I don't want to suggest that the media parenting behaviors I'm recommending will prevent bullying in all its forms, because, as I said, there are so many factors that contribute to aggressive behaviors, such as bullying. But according to the research I've cited here, I feel safe in saying that it appears that reducing children's risky Internet use has the potential to reduce susceptibility to cyberbullying. Too many kids are hurt because of bullying in its various forms, and if there is something I can do to help my kids, even in some small way, it's worth every effort.

### Educational/Prosocial Content

Now, just as we finished the last chapter on a positive note by talking about educational and prosocial content, let's finish this chapter by returning to some media effects that are a little more heartwarming.

First, research shows that exposure to educational media can help improve children's literacy skills. In one study[59] involving 164 kindergarteners and first graders in the Kansas City metro area, some kids watched

17 episodes of *Between the Lions* in their classrooms at school, while other kids maintained their usual nonviewing classroom schedule. The study found that kindergarteners who watched *Between the Lions* performed almost four times better on measures of phonemic awareness (the "awareness that words are made up of sounds"), letter-sound correspondences (the ability to link letters with the sounds they make), and concepts of print (such as knowing that we "read from left to right and top to bottom").[60] They were also better able to identify letters, and they scored higher on reading ability than their classmates who did not watch the show.

The amount of time spent viewing educational programming appears to make a difference when it comes to children's emerging literacy skills. Researchers have concluded that a "moderate" amount of watching TV seems to help kids the most.[61] In other words, small amounts and large (more than three or four hours) amounts of exposure to educational programming that targets early literacy skills do not seem to be as effective as "moderate" amounts. Perhaps even cooler, though, is that viewing educational programs such as *Sesame Street* during the preschool years is related to higher English grades and reading ability, and to reading more books when kids reach adolescence. In other words, exposure to moderate amounts of programming aimed at helping kids develop early literacy skills can have a significant long-term impact on children's academic performance.

Educational television programming can also influence children's language development. For example, in one study[62] involving 236 children ages 2–4, parents reported the names of programs their children watched on the previous day throughout a 3-year period (about 18 reports). The programs were then classified as educational (cartoon and noncartoon), noneducational children's cartoons, other noneducational children's programming, and general-audience programming. Children also periodically met with a researcher so their vocabulary and other skills could be assessed. The study found that children who watched more programming that was categorized as "educational" scored higher on vocabulary tests than children who were infrequent viewers of educational programming. Frequent viewers of each of the other types of programming tended to perform worse, or at least no better, on vocabulary tests than less frequent viewers. Said differently, among all the types of television programming that children watched during the study, the only type of programming that helped children's vocabulary skills was educational programming. This shows once again that content matters.

One educational program in particular not only helped children's vocabulary, but helped children develop a certain set of skills commonly targeted by educational media—prosocial skills. *Blue's Clues* was launched in the mid-90s and had perhaps the best 5–6 year run ever for a children's educational TV show. Before she produced *Daniel Tiger's Neighborhood*, Angela Santomero first created *Blue's Clues*. *Blue's Clues*, as you know, featured an animated dog named Blue and one live actor, Steve. The show, in contrast to *Sesame Street* and all sorts of other programming, took a deliberately slow approach to teaching kids. In his book *Tipping Point*, Malcolm Gladwell described shows that keep children's attention and facilitate their learning as "sticky." The goal of educational programming, then, is to get the information to stick. Due in part to the slow, deliberate nature of *Blue's Clues*, and the way that the show talked directly to children and facilitated interaction with them, Gladwell said, "*Blue's Clues* may be one of the stickiest television shows ever made."[63] A comprehensive study on the effectiveness of *Blue's Clues*, led by University of Alabama researcher Dr. Jennings Bryant, found that exposure to *Blue's Clues* not only significantly improved children's vocabulary, but it contributed to substantial gains in children's problem-solving abilities and flexible-thinking skills (such as being able to see things from multiple points of view).[64] What's more, kids who watched *Blue's Clues* were rated as showing more interest in helping others.

Another of Santomero's "kids" (as she calls the shows she's worked on), is *Daniel Tiger's Neighborhood*. Research shows that this show can help kids develop social skills. When I first started working at Texas Tech University, I started looking around for others on campus with an interest in both media and children's development. I gathered a team of researchers with expertise in both communication and children's socio-emotional development. As we got to know each other during our first meeting, we happened to be talking about shows that our kids watch, and *Daniel Tiger's Neighborhood* seemed to stick out as a favorite. So, I contacted researchers at Out of the Blue Enterprises, Santomero's production company in New York City. With their assistance, and the assistance of The Fred Rogers' Company (yes, that Mister Rogers), we designed a study to test the effectiveness of *Daniel Tiger's Neighborhood* at teaching social skills to children.[65] We enrolled 127 preschoolers ages 2–6 and had some of them watch *Daniel Tiger's Neighborhood*, while others watched a nature show as the "control" condition. The study found that children who watched 10 episodes of *Daniel Tiger's Neighborhood* over a 2-week period exhibited higher levels of empathy, social self-efficacy (confidence in social situations), and ability to recognize emotions than children who did not watch the show. Interestingly, these results were dependent on parents' regular conversations with their kids about educational TV, a topic we'll look at in-depth in an upcoming chapter.

Educational programming has been shown to help kids develop a host of other skills. For example, both *Square One TV* and *Cyberchase* helped kids have more positive attitudes toward math. Children who watched *Square One TV* were also better at forming more sophisticated, or unique, solutions to math problems. And several shows have been found to improve children's comprehension of scientific topics, including *3-2-1 Contact, Bill Nye the Science Guy*, and *The Magic School Bus*.[66] And though I don't know of any research yet that looks at the educational value of *Wild Kratts*, if what my youngest daughter knows about animals is any indication, the show is doing a fantastic job of increasing children's interest in and knowledge about animals.

## Conclusion

Now that we have a better idea of what happens to children when they are exposed to various types of media and media content, it's time to talk about *why* children are affected by media exposure. Knowing that kids are affected is one thing, but if we as parents want to be able to alter those effects, it is essential that we understand *why* kids are affected by media exposure. Let me demonstrate the difference here with an analogy. I know that when I push the gas pedal in my car, the car will go forward. It's cause and effect. Going faster is the effect of pushing the gas pedal. If someday I pushed the gas pedal and the car didn't go faster, I would have to understand why in order to fix the problem. Mechanics understand why, which is why they can charge big bucks for fixing cars. Parents need to understand why their children are affected by media if they want to help be part of the solution. So, now we turn to the science behind media effects on children.

Notes

1.  Craig Anderson and Karen Dill, "Video Games and Aggressive Thoughts, Feelings, and Behavior in the Laboratory and in Life," *Journal of Personality and Social Psychology* 78, no. 4 (2000): 772-790, doi: 10.1037//0022-3514.78.4.772.

2.  Chris Boyatzis, Gina Matillo, and Kristen Nesbitt, "Effects of the 'Mighty Morphin Power Rangers' on Children's Aggression With Peers," *Child Study Journal* 25, no. 1 (1995): 45-55, https://eric.ed.gov/?id=EJ508796.

3.  Children's acts of aggression were coded, or categorized, by researchers.

4. Brad Bushman and L. Rowell Huesmann, "Short-term and Long-term Effects of Violent Media on Aggression in Children and Adults," *Archives of Pediatrics and Adolescent Medicine* 160 (2006): 348-352, doi: 10.1001/archpedi.160.4.348.

5. Hilde Himmelweit, Abraham Oppenheim, and Pamela Vince, *Television and the Child: An Empirical Study of the Effect of Television on the Young,* (New York: Oxford University Press, 1958).

6. Lyle Schramm and Edwin Parker, *Television in the Lives of Our Children* (Stanford, CA: Stanford University Press, 1961).

7. Dave Grossman and Gloria DeGaetano, *Stop Teaching Our Kids to Kill: A Call to Action Against TV, Movie and Video Game Violence* (New York: Crown, 1999).

8. Victor Strasburger, Barbara Wilson, and Amy Jordan, *Children, Adolescents, and the Media*, 3rd ed., (Thousand Oaks, CA: Sage, 2014), 202.

9. Deborah Fisher et al., "Televised Sexual Content and Parental Mediation: Influences on Adolescent Sexuality," *Media Psychology* 12, no. 2 (2009): 121-147, doi: 10.1080/15213260902849901.

10. Participants responded to a survey asking them how much television they watch, how often they watch certain shows that contain high amounts of sexual content, their sexual behaviors, their sexual intentions, and their expectations of the consequences of sexual intercourse. They reported lower expectations of the negative consequences of participating in sexual intercourse.

11. L. Monique Ward and Kimberly Friedman, "Using TV as a Guide: Associations Between Television Viewing and Adolescents' Sexual Attitudes and Behavior," *Journal of Research on Adolescence* 16, no. 1 (2006): 133-156, doi: 10.11111/j.532-7795.2006.00125.x.

12. Jochen Peter, "Media and Sexual Development," in *The Routledge International Handbook of Children, Adolescents and Media,* ed. Dafna Lemish (New York: Routledge, 2015), 217-223.

13. Eric Rasmussen and Rebecca Densley, "Girl in a Country Song: Gender Roles and Objectification of Women in Popular Country Music Across 1990 to 2014," *Sex Roles* 76, (2017): 188-201, doi: 10.1007/s11199-016-0670-6.

14. Margaret McGladrey, "Becoming Tween Bodies: What Preadolescent Girls in the US Say About Beauty, The "Just-Right Ideal," and the "Disney Girls," *Journal of Children and Media* 8, no. 4 (2014): 353-370, doi: 10.1080/17482798.2013.805305.

15. Ibid.

16. Eric Rasmussen, Rebecca Ortiz, and Shawna White, "Emerging Adults' Responses to Active Mediation of Pornography During Adolescence," *Journal of Children and Media* 9, no. 2 (2015): 163-164, doi: 10.1080/17482798.2014.997769.

17. Paul Wright et al., "Pornography Consumption and Satisfaction: A Meta-Analysis," *Human Communication Research* 43, no. 3 (2017): 315-343, doi: 10.1111/hcre.12108.

18. Jane Brown and Kelly L'Engle, "X-rated: Sexual Attitudes and Behaviors Associated With U.S. Early Adolescents' Exposure to Sexually Explicit Media," *Communication Research* 36, no. 1 (2009): 129-151, doi: 10.1177/0093650208326465.

19. Gert Hald, Neil Malamuth, and Carlin Yuen, "Pornography and Attitudes Supporting Violence Against Women: Revisiting the Relationship in Nonexperimental Studies," *Aggressive Behavior* 36, no. 1 (2010): 14-20, doi: 10.1002/ab.20328.

20. Todd Morrison, Shannon Ellis, Melanie Morrison, Anomi Bearden, and Rebecca Harriman, "Exposure to Sexually Explicit Material and Variations in Body Esteem, Genital Attitudes, and Sexual Esteem Among a Sample of Canadian Men," *The Journal of Men's Studies* 14, no. 2 (2006): 209-222, doi: 10.3149/jms.1402.209.

21. Jochen Peter and Patti Valkenburg, "Adolescents' Exposure to Sexually Explicit Internet Material, Sexual Uncertainty, and Attitudes Toward Uncommitted Sexual Exploration: Is There a Link?" *Communication Research* 35, no. 5 (2006): 579-601, doi: 10.1007/s10508-010-9644-x.

22. Jochen Peter and Patti Valkenburg, "Adolescents' Exposure to a Sexualized Media Environment and Their Notions of Women as Sex Objects," *Sex Roles* 56, no. 5-6 (2007): 381-395, doi: 10.1007/s11199-006-9176-y.

23. Dolf Zillmann, "Influence of Unrestrained Access to Erotica on Adolescents' and Young Adults' Dispositions Toward Sexuality," *Journal of Adolescent Health* 27, no. 2 (2000): 41-44, doi: 10.1016/S1054-139X(00)00137-3.

24. Ross Gordon, Anne MacKintosh, and Crawford Moodie, "The Impact of Alcohol Marketing on Youth Drinking Behaviour: A Two-Stage Cohort Study," *Alcohol and Alcoholism* 45, no. 5 (2010): 470-480, doi: 10.1093/alcalc/agq047.

25. Participants completed a survey asking them questions about their current drinking behavior, their family members' drinking behaviors, demographic variables such as age, gender, and religion, as well as questions about their exposure to alcohol marketing in a variety of platforms (TV, billboards, in-store, online, etc.). About two years later, 552 of the same participants responded to the same questions.

26. Jerry Grenard, Clyde Dent, and Alan Stacy, "Exposure to Alcohol Advertisements and Teenage Alcohol-Related Problems," *Pediatrics* 131, no. 2 (2013): doi: 10.1542/peds.2012-1480.

27. "College Drinking," *National Institute on Alcohol Abuse and Alcoholism*, accessed June 21, 2017, http://www.niaaa.nih.gov/alcohol-health/special-populations-co-occurring-disorders/college-drinking.

28. Alan Berkowitz, "An Overview of the Social Norms Approach," in *Changing the Culture of College Drinking: A Socially Situated Health Communication Campaign,* eds. Linda Lederman and Lea Stewart, (Cresskill, NJ: Hampton Press, 2005), 193-214.

29. Ibid.

30. Judith McCool, Becky Freeman, and Helen Tanielu, "Perceived Social and Media Influences on Tobacco Use Among Samoan Youth," *BMC Public Health* 14, no. 1100 (2014): doi: 10.1186/1471-2458-14-1100.

31. *National Survey of American Attitudes on Substance Abuse XVII: Teens*, (New York: The National Center on Addiction and Substance Abuse at Columbia University, 2012).

32. Strasburger, Wilson, and Jordan, "Children, Adolescents, and the Media," 289-290.

33. "The Role of the Media in Promoting and Reducing Tobacco Use," *National Cancer Institute*, accessed June 22, 2017, http://cancercontrol.cancer.gov/brp/tcrb/monographs/19/docs/M19MajorConclusionsFactSheet.pdf.

34. Annemarie Charlesworth and Stanton Glantz, "Smoking in the Movies Increases Adolescent Smoking: A Review," *Pediatrics* 116, no. 6 (2005): 1516-1528, doi: 10.1542/peds.2005-0141.

35. Benjamin Alamar and Stanton Glantz, "Tobacco Industry Profits From Smoking Images in the Movies," *Pediatrics* 117, no. 4 (2006): 1462, doi: 10.1542/peds.2005-3088.

36. Amy Slater and Marika Tiggemann, "Little Girls in a Grown Up World: Exposure to Sexualized Media, Internalization of Sexualization Messages, and Body Image in 6-9 Year-Old Girls," *Body Image* 18, (2016): 19-22, doi: 10.1016/j.bodyim.2016.04.004.

37. Researchers showed the girls drawings of a girl wearing 6 different outfits, each a little more provocative than the last, and asked girls to point to the outfits (1) that look like the ones they wear, (2) that they like, (3) that are popular, and (4) that they think boys like best on girls. Girls were also asked to point to 1 of 9 female silhouettes that they think most looks like them and which they would most like to look like, the difference being the size of their "body dissatisfaction."

38. Juliet Schor, *Born to Buy: The Commercialized Child and the New Commercial Culture* (New York: Scribner, 2004), 11.

39. Jennifer Harris, John Bargh, and Kelly Brownell, "Priming Effects of Television Food Advertising on Eating Behavior," *Health Psychology* 28, no. 4 (2009): 404-413, doi: 10.1037/a0014399.

40. *Set of Recommendations on the Marketing of Foods and Non-Alcoholic Beverages to Children*, (Switzerland: World Health Organization, 2010), 4, http://apps.who.int/iris/bitstream/10665/44416/1/9789241500210_eng.pdf.

41. Ibid., 5

42. Moniek Buijzen and Patti Valkenburg, "The Impact of Television Advertising on Children's Christmas Wishes," *Journal of Broadcasting & Electronic Media* 44, no. 3 (2000): 456-470, doi: 10.1207/s15506878jobem4403_7.

43. Children were presented with a list of 12 popular Saturday morning children's programs on 2 popular commercial children's networks and were asked to report how much they watch the shows. Commercials during the shows were

recorded over several weeks, and the content of the commercials was compiled and analyzed.

44. Simone de Droog, Patti Valkenburg, and Moniek Buijzen, "Using Brand Characters to Promote Young Children's Liking of and Purchase Requests for Fruit," *Journal of Health Communication* 16, no. 1 (2010): 79-89, doi: 10.1080/1080730.2010.529487.

45. Strasburger, Wilson, & Jordan, "Children, Adolescents, and the Media," 73-74.

46. Holly Henry and Dina Borzekowski, "The Nag Factor: A Mixed-Methodology Study in the US of Young Children's Requests for Advertised Products," *Journal of Children and Media* 5, no. 3 (2011): 298-317, doi: 10.1080/17482798.2011.584380.

47. Craig Anderson et al., "Violent Video Game Effects on Aggression, Empathy, and Prosocial Behavior in Eastern and Western Countries: A Meta-Analytic Review," *Psychological Bulletin* 136, no. 2 (2010): 151-173, doi: 10.1037/a0018251.

48. Douglas Gentile et al., "The Effects of Prosocial Video Games on Prosocial Behaviors: International Evidence From Correlational, Longitudinal, and Experimental Studies," *Personality and Social Psychology Bulletin* 35, no. 6 (2009): 752-763, doi: 10.1177/0146167209333045.

49. David Ewoldsen et al., "Effect of Playing Violent Video Games Cooperatively or Competitively on Subsequent Cooperative Behavior," *Cyberpsychology, Behavior, and Social Networking* 15, no. 5 (2012): 277-280, doi: 10.1089/cyber.2011.0308.

50. Nikolina Banjanin et al., "Relationship Between Internet Use and Depression: Focus on Physiological Mood Oscillations, Social Networking and Online Addictive Behavior," *Computers in Human Behavior* 43 (2015): 308-312, doi: 10.1016/j.chb.2014.11.013.

51. Igor Pantic et al., "Association Between Online Social Networking and Depression in High School Students: Behavioral Physiology Viewpoint," *Psychiatria Danubina* 24, no. 1 (2012): 90-93, www.hdbp.org/psychiatria_danubina/pdf/dnb_vol24_no1/dnb_vol24_no1_90.pdf.

52. Kathryn Yung et al., "Internet Addiction Disorder and Problematic Use of Google Glass in Patient Treated at a Residential Substance Abuse Treatment Program," *Addictive Behaviors* 41 (2015): 58-60, doi: 10.1016/j.addbeh.2014.09.024.

53. David Smahel, Michelle Wright, and Martina Cernikova, "The Impact of Digital Media on Health: Children's Perspectives," *International Journal of Public Health* 60, no. 2 (2015): 131-137, doi: 10.1007/s00038-015-0649-z.

54. For a review, see Atika Khurana et al., "The Protective Effects of Parental Monitoring and Internet Restriction on Adolescents' Risk of Online Harassment," *Journal of Youth and Adolescence* 44, no. 5 (2015): 1039-1047, doi: 10.1007/s10964-014-0242-4.

55. Elisabeth Staksrud, Kjartan Ólafsson, and Sonia Livingstone, "Does the Use of Social Networking Sites Increase Children's Risk of Harm?" *Computers in Human Behavior* 29, no. 1 (2013): 40-50, doi: 10.1016/j.chb.2012.05.026.

56. H. Chahal et al., "Availability and Night-Time Use of Electronic Entertainment and Communication Devices are Associated With Short Sleep Duration and Obesity Among Canadian Children," *Pediatric Obesity* 8 (2013): 42-51, doi: 10.1111/j.2047-6310.2012.00085.x.

57. Lisa Jones, Kimberly Mitchell, and David Finkelhor, "Trends in Youth Internet Victimization: Findings From Three Youth Internet Safety Surveys 2000-2010," *Journal of Adolescent Health*, 50, no. 2 (2011): 179-186, doi: 10.1016/j.jadohealth.2011.09.015.

58. Liang Chen, Shirley Ho, and May Lwin, "A Meta-Analysis of Factors Predicting Cyberbullying Perpetration and Victimization: From the Social Cognitive and Media Effects Approach," *New Media & Society* (2016), doi: 10.1177/1461444816634037.

59. Deborah Linebarger, *Summative Evaluation of Between the Lions: A Final Report to WGBH Educational Foundation*. (Kansas City: University of Kansas, 2000), 1-109.

60. Ibid., 2.

61. Annie Moses, "Impacts of Television Viewing on Young Children's Literacy Development in the USA: A Review of the Literature," *Journal of Early Childhood Literacy* 8, no. 1 (2008): 67-102, doi: 10.1177/1468798407162.

62. John Wright et al., "The Relations of Early Television Viewing to School Readiness and Vocabulary of Children From Low-Income Families: The Early Window Project," *Child Development* 72, no. 5 (2001): 1347-1366, www.andrews.edu/~rbailey/Chapter%2014/5548963.pdf.

63. Malcolm Gladwell. *The Tipping Point: How Little Things Can Make a Big Difference.* (New York: Little, Brown and Company, 2002), 112.

64. Daniel Anderson et al., "Researching Blue's Clues: Viewing Behavior and Impact," *Media Psychology* 2, no. 2 (2000): 179-194, doi: 10.1207/S1532785XMEP0202_4.

65. Eric Rasmussen et al., "Relation Between Active Mediation, Exposure to Daniel Tiger's Neighborhood, and US Preschoolers' Social and Emotional Development," *Journal of Children and Media* 10, no. 4 (2016): 443-461, doi: 10.1080/17482798.2016.1203806.

66. For a review, see Shalom Fisch, *Children's Learning From Educational Television: Sesame Street and Beyond* (New York: Routledge, 2014).

# 4 The Science behind Media Effects

Even more essential than understanding media exposure's effect on us and on our children, is *why* it has an effect. To help our kids make it through the media maze, parents need to understand why the maze works the way it does. In this chapter, we'll explore a few of my favorite theories that help explain how and why media exposure affects us the way it does. This chapter is in no way exhaustive or comprehensive of media effects theories—there are textbooks for that. And you should know that each researcher tends to gravitate to their favorite theories. The theories I've chosen to focus on in this chapter are generally referred to by researchers as priming, cultivation, social cognitive theory, social norms, and limited cognitive capacity. So, let's crack open the human mind just a little bit and see the cognitive mechanisms and processes at work when people consume media.

If you're a parent, you're likely reading this book because you believe that media has an effect on kids. In the previous chapter, we reviewed some of the research that confirmed your hunch. But why does media have an effect? How does it work? Media content is not like a pill from the pharmacy—there isn't necessarily a dose-response relationship. To use the human body as a metaphor, most bodies work about the same. My body has organs, limbs, white blood cells, amino acids, water, and all sorts of other chemicals in it. With slight variations, your body likely functions about the same as mine. Your lungs breathe in. My lungs breathe in. Your heart beats. My heart beats. That's why we can both go to the pharmacy and pick up a bottle of Ibuprofen and it will help us both get rid of our headaches. It's also why eating too much and exercising too little will likely result in us both becoming overweight. When we talk about the body, we can make predictions with relative assurance about how they will react to certain stimuli, such as food and medicine. This is probably why medical doctors make the big bucks, while we in the social sciences deal with less concrete issues and make less money (but I'm not complaining. Okay, maybe I am a little). Social scientists deal with the mind, with attitudes, with thought processes. I can't give you a pill (at least not an FDA-approved pill) that will cure you of a bad attitude toward your daughter's boyfriend or that will make you like country music. Sure, our minds may be made up of the same stuff, but we're dealing with more than chemicals and medical procedures when dealing with the mind.

For example, my reaction to watching an episode of a popular weight-loss program like *The Biggest Loser*—the stimuli—will be different than your reaction. We each bring different life experiences to our viewing of the show. We bring different genetic propensities for obesity that might affect our perception of stories involving weight loss. But if we're all so different, how can we make any predictions about when and how somebody will be affected by media exposure? The truth is, while we are all completely different, we likely share some unique things in common. Even though we can't make perfect predictions about when and how people will be affected by media exposure, we can make predictions about the likelihood of things happening because of what we know about how the mind processes information.

When I refer to information processing, I'm talking about what happens in our minds when our senses pick up on things happening around us. If I'm driving down the road and I see the traffic light turn yellow, my brain processes that and associates yellow with "slow down." That translates into the behavior of me putting my foot on the brake. The yellow light doesn't make my foot press on the brake, but my appraisal of what should happen when I see the yellow light makes my foot go down. Our minds never stop working, and whether or not we are aware that we're thinking about what we see around us, our minds are taking it in and storing all that information somewhere between our ears. I'll bet you can remember what the weather was like yesterday. You don't need that information anymore today, but somehow your mind stored it somewhere. What color are the shingles on your roof? Even though you don't think you need that information right now, your mind has it stored in there at some level of readiness to retrieve it. Which leads us into the first of the media effects theories that we'll review: priming.

## Media Effects Theory #1: Priming

On my weedwacker, right near the engine, is a little plastic bubble. The instructions for starting the weedwacker say that I need to push the bubble eight times in order to let some of the fuel in. This primes the engine, so to speak. In essence, pushing the bubble on the weedwacker moves some of the fuel closer to where it's needed in order to get the engine up and running. Priming an engine feeds just enough of the fuel into the right spot so that the engine will work. When we speak of media effects, priming theory works in a similar way. Let's illustrate priming with an example involving exposure to sexual media content.

A study led by Dr. Francesca Dillman Carpentier showed that people can be affected by media content through the process of priming.[1] In the study, each of 60 college student participants were told they would be evaluating Internet sites. After evaluating a few sites, participants listened to 3.5 minutes of popular music under the guise that music had the ability to clear their heads for the second half of the study. The songs were performed by either Madonna or Janet Jackson and were either sexually suggestive or not. After listening to 3.5 minutes of sexual or nonsexual songs, each participant saw three profiles of single people of the opposite sex from a fictitious dating website. The profiles included the person's name and a written description of the person's interests. Each participant then rated each profile on a scale of 1–10 in eight different categories including sensitive, assertive, sexy, dependable, aggressive, desirable, sincere, and impulsive. A last question asked participants how attracted to the person they would be if they actually met them, on a scale of 1–10. The results were fascinating. Participants who listened to the sexually suggestive music rated the people in the profiles as more sexually desirable than those who listened to the songs with innocuous lyrics.

Priming theory would suggest that exposure to sexual lyrics, even for a brief period of time, subconsciously activated certain concepts in the minds of the listeners. When those concepts were activated in the person's mind, they subsequently influenced the unrelated ratings of dating site profiles. In other words, the sexual lyrics primed the pump. The lyrics brought the idea of sexuality to the forefront of the listeners' minds without them even knowing it, and when ideas are brought to the front of the mind, they tend to influence our responses to information in our environment. It should be noted here that priming research suggests that these effects are extraordinarily short term, in that they don't last very long. At the same time, however, priming research suggests that the more an idea is primed—brought to the front of the mind—the more likely it is to come to the front of the mind in the future. Ideas that are close to the front of the mind are described as "accessible." Our memory can easily access them. Ultimately, ideas can be "chronically accessible," meaning they are always at or near the surface of a person's thoughts. If that is the case, you can see how repeated exposure to sexual lyrics, or other sexual media content, can influence how we see people, including a spouse, girlfriend or boyfriend, daughter or son, friend, coworkers, and others. To say it another way, the more a person is exposed to certain media content, such as sexual content, the more that content biases the way that person views the world. We tend to see the world through the lens of the thoughts that are nearest the surface in our mind.

Let's take this idea of priming just a bit further now. Dr. Carpentier conducted a follow-up study several years later.[2] Like the previous study, participants listened to either sexually suggestive music or nonsexual music in order to "clear their heads" for about three minutes. They were then asked to evaluate the résumés of three purported on-campus job candidates, as if they were involved in the hiring process. Among the attributes they evaluated were how racy, flirtatious, and rebellious they thought the job candidate was. Like the previous study, those who listened to sexual music rated the job applicants as possessing more sexual qualities. What's more, results found that these ratings of sexuality, in turn, predicted the rater's overall rating of the job candidate's character. In other words, listening to sexual music lyrics once again brought the idea of sexuality to the forefront of listeners' minds, but this time, the research showed that these sexual thoughts were then used in evaluating the character of a person that they had never before met.

As you can see, priming is a powerful explanation for how media exposure may affect us in our everyday lives, without us even knowing it. Granted, the studies I've referred to included adult (college students) participants. Can you imagine, however, how kids might then be affected in this way? I suppose one of two things could happen. Because kids have less life experience, the sexual content could cause the idea of sexuality to dominate their perceptions of others, simply because they have less life experience to suggest that others may have qualities besides their sexuality that should be considered. On the other hand, because children have not spent a lifetime being exposed to sexual content, it is possible that these priming effects aren't strong enough to affect their perceptions until they have listened to enough of it to make a difference. Future research could help us parse these possibilities apart.

Let me share just one more example of how priming, or the accessibility of our thoughts, biases our views of what goes on around us. It's a football analogy, so for you nonfootball fans, bear with me here. In early 2003, Ohio State and Miami met in the college football national championship game. The game went into overtime. It was fourth down and Ohio State had one last chance to send the game into double overtime. They threw a pass into the end zone that was dropped. Miami players and fans started to celebrate, but Ohio State fans went crazy calling for a pass interference penalty on the Miami defender. The referees huddled together and eventually called a pass interference penalty on Miami. Miami fans couldn't believe it. Ohio State fans said the referees got the call right. Ohio State was awarded another play and went on to win the game. To this day, there is disagreement between fans of the two schools about what the right call was on the play. How can two groups of people who saw the same football play have seen it so differently? The answer lies in how "top of mind" their feelings for their school were. The more of a Miami fan a viewer was, the more likely they were to have not seen the pass interference. The more of an Ohio State fan a viewer was, the more likely they were to have seen the pass interference. It's a matter of perception, driven by the biases created by exposure after exposure to messages about the greatness of their respective school.

What does this mean for your kids then? This suggests that the less our children are exposed to undesirable media content, such as sexual media content, the less chance there is of their perceptions of the world being biased, or clouded, by the messages contained in the media. The less the engine is primed, the harder it will be to get it started. But the more the engine is primed, the more easily it will run. For example, a violent television program could "prime" aggressive thoughts in child viewers, leading them to react aggressively to a subsequent disagreement. This could explain how watching *Karate Kid* influenced my subsequent punching of my younger brother. Perhaps my thoughts had been primed with aggressive thoughts, which led me to resolve a situation through aggression, where if I hadn't recently seen *Karate Kid*, I might have handled the situation in a less aggressive manner. The less someone is exposed to certain content, the harder it will be to bring those thoughts to the forefront of the mind, which could reduce the likelihood that those thoughts will guide one's perceptions of people, situations, and one's daily life experiences.

## Media Effects Theory #2: Cultivation

My wife is a beautiful woman, inside and out. She is an amazing writer, editor, and thinker. She is also good at a lot of other things—parenting, befriending others, and being patient with our kids. And with me. I'm not sure another woman has ever had to practice as much patience with a husband as she has with me. But bless her heart, she does not have a green thumb. Over the years, she has been unable to keep a host of plants alive. At its root, the word "cultivation" hearkens to the care and tending needed to raise plants. Whether it's her lack of cultivation skills, or that plants just don't seem to like her, taking care of plants—cultivating them—just hasn't historically been in my wife's skillset. That doesn't change the way I feel about her. It just means I get to do more of the yard work. And since I love the smell of freshly cut grass, I usually don't mind.

The idea of cultivation has also been applied to media use. The premise of cultivation theory is that the more one consumes media, especially television content, the more one will view the real world as being similar to the televised world. For example, let's revisit the idea of the thin ideal that we discussed in a previous chapter. Researchers have analyzed the content of popular television programming and have determined that television portrays a "thin ideal." That is, women on television are remarkably thinner than the average woman in real life. One study found that about 30% of female characters on television are underweight, compared to 5% in real life.[3] Conversely, about half of the women in the United States are considered overweight, but only 13% of female characters on television are considered overweight. This is also true for media directed at children. Another study looked at Disney animated films over a 60-year period and found that female Disney characters who were thin were rated as more "good."[4] The ideal woman, as portrayed in the media, has small hips, a small waist, and relatively large, but not overly large, breasts.[5, 6] From infancy, then, girls are subjected to a distorted view of what a typical female looks like. In fact, the message is incessant and prevalent in all forms of media. Exposure to the media's thin ideal is related to females' desire to be slimmer and to being dissatisfied with their body, leading to concern about disordered eating and even mental disorders such as anorexia.[7] And perhaps not surprisingly, such internalization of the thin ideal appears to occur during late childhood and early adolescence,[8] the exact time at which body changes already cause anxiety among girls.

Cultivation is one explanation for why the thin ideal has these effects. Cultivation theory would say that the more girls are exposed to the thin ideal, the more they think that the typical woman is, or should be, thin-waisted and big-busted. Over time, the media cultivates these thoughts just as water and sun cultivate a seed. Girls then look at themselves in the mirror and make comparisons between their body and what they think an attractive female should look like. Of course, they feel inadequate. Of course, they feel fat and less attractive. As a father of four daughters, this is extremely frustrating, especially since media is pervasive and ever-present in our society—no matter how much I try to reduce their exposure to media, they will still be exposed to the thin ideal. It's on billboards, in magazines, on social media, everywhere. But, remember, a basic tenet of cultivation theory is that *heavy* exposure is the real culprit. This means that if exposure to the thin ideal is reduced to a level that is below *heavy*, then cultivation effects should be less. So, yes, there is hope. Understanding cultivation theory should give you both pause and hope at the same time.

Cultivation theory, in my opinion, is highly related to our previous discussion of priming. If we are constantly exposed to a message, such as the thin ideal, priming theory would suggest that it becomes more top of mind, more accessible in our memory. Remember that what is top of mind tends to guide our attitudes and our behaviors. So, it makes sense that the more we watch television, the more we perceive the world in which we live as similar to the televised world.

Cultivation theory also helps explain what social scientists call the "mean world syndrome." Research shows that watching television news is related to the belief that young people are committing an increasing amount of crime.[9] This means that the more we view news about crime or watch crime dramas, the more violent we will think the world is. In other words, because television shows are chock-full of violence, we begin to see the world as an increasingly violent place. We may begin to think that people are less kind, that others are out to get us, that everybody is simply motivated by a survival-of-the-fittest mentality. But think about it, news is news because it is an anomaly. Child abductions make the news because they are rare. Bank robberies make the news because they don't happen very often. The same goes for train derailments, large tornadoes, earthquakes in highly populated areas, tsunamis, and all the things we see or read about in the news. Logically, we know this is the case, but cultivation theory says that our knowledge about the truth of the frequency of bad things happening is not strong enough to override the subconscious perception that these things happen all the time because that is all we see on the news.

This makes me wonder what would happen if there was a news channel solely devoted to sharing good news. In the car on the way to school on many mornings, my kids and I listen to the *Bobby Bones* radio show. The show has a segment that focuses solely on good news, on the good things that people do. Cultivation theory would suggest that if we were exposed to heavy amounts of such good news, we would think the world is much safer than it actually is, that people are more altruistic than they really are, and that bad things never happen to good people. Some of the coolest research about media effects recently has focused on this. Dr. Mary Beth Oliver is a highly respected media researcher at Penn State University. She is leading a line of research showing that some media exposure may result in what she calls a "kind world syndrome."[10] For example, Dr. Oliver talked about a study she's conducting in which she gave Penn State students a photo challenge. She asked them to take photos of beauty or kindness in their lives. Combined with some of her other research, she's convinced that it's possible to help people believe that the world is a good place by helping them pay more attention to the good and the beautiful around them. In an interview at Penn State, she said, "Professionally, I think the media is accused of doing pretty bad things in our society—and for good reason. There is a lot of ugly content, but at the same time I see that there's much more than that. We owe it to ourselves to really look at not just stopping the bad, but exposing the good. Personally, when I witness media's portrayals of beauty, I am elevated. It's possible to heighten people's feelings and connectedness."[11]

What if television depicted reality as it really is? Well, watching the news would be boring because it would basically be a replay of our mostly mundane, day-to-day lives. Maybe we'd notice a little more good and a little less bad. So, I guess that as long as media owners can make money off of media, the rare, negative occurrences of life will populate the news and we will tend to have a negatively skewed, distorted view of what the world is really like. That's cultivation.

## Media Effects Theory #3: Social Cognitive Theory

For most of human history on this planet, we have not had access to information via mass media. It is believed that the first civilizations that used writing extensively were the Sumerians or the Egyptians around 3,400–3,200 BC. They wrote using symbols on clay tablets, woven papyrus plants, animal hides, pressed wood, and fiber pulp. Paper wasn't invented until around 3,000 BC, but by no means was this early form of communication easily distributed to the masses. Until the invention of the movable type printing press by Johannes Gutenberg in the 1400s, communication was largely oral in nature or was done by way of slow and costly hand-copying. This means that what people knew about the world was largely confined to what they could learn from relatively few people in a limited geographic area. I don't think it is coincidence that the long period known as the Dark Ages occurred prior to the advent of the movable type printing press. It was before this invention that people had limited access to information beyond their immediate surroundings.

This brief discussion about the history of communication is important to our understanding of what social cognitive theory is. Social cognitive theory encompasses a lot about how we as humans learn. As it pertains to the media, social cognitive theory says that we learn about the world, about how to think and behave, about social norms and rules, from watching others. In other words, we learn vicariously through observing the experiences of others. In the pre-printing press era, the opportunities for vicarious learning were, as we have stated, limited to a relatively small group of people in a small geographic area. The invention of the printing press didn't change how people learn from others, but it introduced vast amounts of previously inaccessible information into the lives of people. And because we learn from observing others' experiences, mass media introduced endless opportunities to learn from others' experiences.

Let's continue this discussion of the history of communication as I understand it for just a bit longer. Someday after I die and I get to wherever it is I'm going, I hope I end up in the same place as Johannes Guttenberg, because he is one of my heroes. What he did changed the course of history. Before the invention of his printing press, religious texts were managed and read primarily by literate members of the clergy. Literacy was low outside of the clergy ranks. But because of the printing press, lay people gained access to religious texts such as the Bible. Because of their access to the Bible, people started reading and interpreting it for themselves. The Protestant Reformation was ignited. Martin Luther's 95 theses posted on the door of All Saints' Church in Wittenberg, Germany, in 1517 came as a result, presumably, of his reading of the Bible, which was made possible by the printing press. The Reformation made its way to England where a small group of people decided to break away from the Church of England and charter a boat called the Mayflower. Upon arrival in the New World, these people set the foundation for a Constitution that would guarantee the right to worship as one pleases—a right that had not existed to such an extent in much of the world's history. I share all of this simply to show that exposure to mass media changes people, and ultimately, society. And these changes often occur because of how we learn.

We won't get into all the minutiae of social cognitive theory, but part of the theory suggests that we learn through observation. If we didn't learn through observation, we could only learn through personal experiences. We would never learn that touching a hot stove can burn our hand unless we tried it for ourselves. We would never learn the consequences of driving a car into a brick wall unless we were behind the wheel when it happened. A moral to the story would be pointless because it would mean nothing to us since we couldn't personally experience it. How awful would that be? But, because we can learn vicariously through observing others, we can learn to avoid certain behaviors simply because they turned out bad for another person. For example, I grew up with a dad who was a carpenter and homebuilder. He told me on many occasions that the reason he doesn't hit his thumb with a hammer was because it hurts too bad, and because he can't stand seeing all the blood. I've seen people hit their thumb with a hammer and cause serious damage. I learned from that and try to avoid hitting my thumb whenever I use a hammer, because I don't want to experience the associated pain. I didn't have to hit my thumb with a hammer to know that it would hurt, because I learned vicariously through my dad. Similarly, I learned that certain behaviors resulted in certain desirable and undesirable consequences simply because I had an older brother and an older sister whom I could watch and learn from.

And so it is with mass media. We can learn to paint by watching Bob Ross. We can learn to cook by watching Julia Child. This observational learning can help us navigate our worlds in so many positive ways. But based on what you know about media content, can you see how this way of learning can be detrimental? If media rarely portrays the negative consequences of violent or risky behavior, there is less opportunity to learn that these behaviors can result in bad outcomes. In addition, if violence is glamorized and justified in the media, we will learn by observation that employing violence and risky behaviors in real life may be likewise glamorized and justified. Now, obviously, learning is not as clean as this, but you get the picture. Our ability to learn vicariously could help explain why people who are exposed to large amounts of sexual content that fails to show the consequences of risky sexual behaviors are more willing to engage in risky sexual behaviors themselves. It is no wonder, then, that behaviors such as premarital cohabitation and premarital bearing of children are on the rise (whether or not you agree with premarital sex or the concept of marriage), that a culture of hooking-up on college campuses is prevalent, and that people engage in sexual behaviors without thinking about the social, emotional, and mental consequences that could come. Because the media doesn't always show all the consequences of these behaviors, some people simply don't learn the consequences until they learn through painful, personal experience, as if they still lived in the Dark Ages.

Research related to media's portrayal of relational aggression helps illustrate this point. Relational aggression includes things like backbiting, gossiping, spreading rumors, and the like. Research has found that children's exposure to relational aggression on television is related to their actual use of relational aggression in real life.[12, 13] I suspect that this is the case because depictions of relational aggression rarely show negative consequences for the person who is relationally aggressive. We learn from such programming that the popular crowd uses relational aggression, that gossiping and making fun of others is funny, and that it's okay to use others for personal gain. Without any outside instruction from parents or others, it makes perfect sense that exposure to relationally aggressive content leads to relational aggression. Note here, however, that I said "without any outside instruction from parents or others." We will soon learn about the role of parents in throwing a wrench into the process of learning vicariously through media exposure.

Social cognitive theory can also be demonstrated by a study with which I was involved led by Dr. Sarah Coyne at Brigham Young University. The study explains that the development of gender in children is in part a result of watching and then modeling the behaviors of others, including parents, peers, teachers, and the media.[14] This modeling tends to be most powerful when the models are attractive and the same gender. The study looked at the power of Disney princesses to engender gender stereotypes. Disney princesses, as you know, are extremely popular among young girls. The Disney princess line—it is a product line, after all—includes around a dozen princesses. Parents generally view the princesses as something safe for girls to be involved with, but others, according to the study, worry that girls learn the message that girls should be passive and need to rely on men in order to be successful. Based on this background, the study tested 198 young children (average age was around 5 years old) at two different points in time. Results showed that the more kids engaged with Disney princesses (watched them on TV/movies, played with Disney princess-related toys, etc.), the more likely they were to adhere to behaviors that are common stereotypes for the female gender. These behaviors included a preference for gender-stereotypical toys, such as dolls and tea sets, and engagement in gender-stereotypical activities, such as playing house and playing dress up. In short, research shows that kids do indeed model the behaviors of characters in the media, lending support for the explanation offered by social cognitive theory.

## Media Effects Theory #4: Social Norms

Closely related to both cultivation theory and social cognitive theory is the idea that media exposure can affect our social norms. A social norm is social science's way of talking about our perceptions of how other people act and think. When we say that we do something because "everyone is doing it," we're really saying that we think the behavior is normal, or that the behavior is a social norm. And even though we like to say we aren't affected by what we think is socially acceptable, we all consistently act in conformance with our social norms. Let's illustrate this with a silly example. I never had an office job until after I was married. I was still an undergraduate, and since I was married, I also felt the pressure that comes with supporting a family. Somehow, I landed a job in the public relations department of a billion-dollar, publicly traded company (even though the cover letter I sent was actually addressed to a different company). Because I'd never had an office job, I also never had an office job wardrobe. So, I bought some khakis and a few button-up shirts, and every day I dressed myself in my new duds, complete with white socks and casual, dark dress shoes.

Did you catch that? Is there something about my wardrobe that sticks out to you as a social faux pas? That's right, white socks. You don't wear white socks with dark dress shoes. It's tacky. But who says so? Why is wearing white socks with dress shoes and pants such a tacky thing to do? It's because society sets this rule that it isn't the most appropriate wardrobe selection. I started paying attention to the other guys at work, and sure enough, I was the only one wearing white socks. So, I gave in. Because I didn't want to be the only "unprofessional" one in the office, I made the switch. Because everybody was doing it, I began to do it too.

When it comes to media, social norms work both ways: norms can affect what we choose to listen to and watch. And vice versa—what we listen to and watch can affect our norms. For example, a survey study asked 810 adolescents how often in the past month they purposely sought out sexual media content.[15] The survey also asked participants about their perceptions of how much their peers purposely sought out sexual media content. From what you know now about the effect of social norms, the results should come as no surprise. Results showed that adolescents' intentions to purposely seek out sexual media content were strongly affected by both how much they thought their peers did so, and by how much they thought their peers approved of seeking out sexual media content. Other research shows that an individual's perception of others' typical behaviors can lead to littering,[16] drinking behavior,[17] and use of marijuana.[18]

Because our norms affect our behaviors, it is important to discover the determinants of our norms. First, norms come from our peer groups. For example, you may have heard of the Asch experiment. In 1951, a researcher named Solomon Asch brought several people into a room together and showed them pictures of straight lines of varying length.[19] Each participant was asked which line was the longest. After the first few trials, several of the people in the room, who were actually researchers in disguise, started agreeing that the longest line was actually one of the shorter lines. By the time the question was asked of the study participants, they figured they must have been doing something wrong and they agreed with the group. Talk about a desire to conform! Our desire to conform, to act in concert with our social norms, is so strong that we will sometimes go with the group even when we know the group is wrong. In fact, social norms are so powerful that *thinking* our peers are doing something affects our behavior even more than whether they are *actually* doing that thing or not.[20]

In addition to peers, media exposure can be a source of information that people use to develop norms. Remember our discussion about cultivation theory? When we consume media content, we develop perceptions about the prevalence of others' behaviors, such as how often adolescents are involved in crime. Social norms theories suggest that when we think others are regularly participating in a behavior, then we are more likely to also participate in that behavior. This should sound familiar. Remember the thin ideal? If women think all women look a certain way, they will begin to think that they have to look that way too. Research shows this to be the case. In a study involving 189 kids ages 13–15, researchers had the participants look at one of two types of Facebook profiles that were fabricated by the researchers.[21] All participants saw profiles of the same four high school students. Some participants viewed profiles of three students that showed them drinking alcohol and one of a student who was not shown drinking, while other participants saw the profiles of three students who were not shown drinking and one of a student who was shown drinking. Results showed that study participants who viewed the profiles showing alcohol drinking as normative (the condition with three students using alcohol) reported greater willingness to drink alcohol, more positive attitudes toward alcohol, and more positive ratings of the people in the alcohol-condition profiles.

Not only, then, is the media a powerful influence on what we think others are doing or thinking, but our belief in the media's power to influence social norms is so strong that even if we think our friends will be affected by certain media messages, we will be more likely to be affected by them, even if our friends aren't actually affected by the messages. A study involving 818 sixth and seventh graders asked participants about their exposure to antismoking and prosmoking media messages.[22] Participants also rated how often they thought their peers saw the same messages and how often they thought their friends and fellow students smoke. The results showed that the more prosmoking messages kids were exposed to, the more they thought their peers were also exposed to prosmoking media messages. And the more kids thought their peers were exposed to prosmoking messages, the more they thought their friends smoked. And the more they thought their friends smoked, the more they reported either smoking or that they intended to smoke.

## Media Effects Theory #5: Limited Cognitive Capacity

When we try to answer the question of "why" or "how" the media affects kids, it is important to remember that kids' minds work differently than adults' minds. We'll end this chapter on a positive note by talking about how media messages can be developed in order to have positive influences on children. To illustrate, let's start with a brief exercise. I'm going to list a set of numbers. I want you to read the numbers and then cover them up and see if you can repeat them backward. For example, if I wrote 2, 4, you would cover up the numbers and say 4, 2. Simple enough, right? Okay, here we go:

3, 13. Cover it up and repeat it backward.
2, 7, 10. Cover it up and repeat in backward.
6, 14, 8, 21. Cover it up and repeat in backward.
1, 12, 17, 4, 9. Cover it up and repeat in backward.
18, 5, 0, 7, 22, 16. Cover it up and repeat in backward.
32, 1, 0, 8, 13, 7, 12. Cover it up and repeat in backward.

You probably noticed that repeating the numbers backward was pretty easy at first, but as the chain of numbers became longer, it became more difficult to do. Here's why. Even though we think we are good at multi-tasking, we can really only think about one thing really well at any given time. In this exercise, we're trying to think of two things—the numbers themselves, and the order in which they were presented. When more information is entered into the exercise, our performance decreases because our minds have a limited capacity to process information. We can only think about so many things at once before what we call "cognitive overload" occurs. When cognitive overload occurs, we forget things, mix things up, and make mistakes. It's like trying to pour water into a cup. When the cup is full, it's full, and it can't hold any more water. If you try to pour more water into a full cup, it will spill over and make a mess. We call our limited mental abilities "cognitive capacity."

The cognitive capacity of adults and children is different. Adults have much higher cognitive capacity. We can hold more information in our working memory at once than children can. What does this have to do with media? Let's use children's television programming as an example. My youngest daughter's favorite TV show is *Wild Kratts*. The show is about two brothers who are fanatic about nature and turn into animals in order to teach kids about the cool things that animals do. When kids watch the show, they are presented with two basic kinds of information: (1) the facts about animals, and (2) the plot, or what researchers call the "narrative." Because of kids' limited ability to think about multiple things at once, it is hard for them to think about the narrative while also thinking about the lesson being taught in the show. But, research shows that when the lesson is interwoven into the plot, children's learning increases. For example, if the Kratt brothers went to the park and played basketball, and a bird landed on a park bench, and then the Kratt brothers started pointing out the features of the bird, children would have to follow the plot about playing basketball and then try to retain the information about the bird's features. This could be difficult for a child. But *Wild Kratts* does something different. In the show, the Kratt brothers become the bird. And because they are the bird, the plot can show how the features of the bird help the brothers accomplish a goal. The lesson and the plot are tightly intertwined. Kids learn better when this is the case because they do not have to devote their limited cognitive resources to two separate things. When the plot and the lesson become one, there is more room in kids' heads to devote to learning the lesson.[23]

## Conclusion

Unlike a clock or a car, we can't take apart the human brain to figure out how it works and then put it back together again. Our minds are malleable. The brain is a living thing, one that can be altered by its environment. It can be trained. It already does some things without us consciously thinking about it. It keeps our hearts beating and lungs breathing. And it works without stopping in an attempt to make sense of the world around us. The brain is constantly processing information that it takes in through our senses. Because the brain can be trained, media messages are able to change how we view the world. How this change happens is still largely a mystery simply because every person is different, but science has given us a glimpse—as I've tried to demonstrate—into how the messages we take in can change us. The trick for parents, then, is twofold. First, it's a parent's job to help kids fill their brains with good stuff. We have to feed their brains well if we want them to behave well. And second, we have to train the brain to deal with the bad stuff that it will encounter. Because kids' brains are still developing, they need help to make the most of the good and to deal with the bad. And nobody is in a better position to do this than parents.

# Notes

1. Francesca Carpentier, Silvia Knobloch-Westerwick, and Andree Blumhoff, "Naughty Versus Nice: Suggestive Pop Music Influences on Perceptions of Potential Romantic Partners," *Media Psychology* 9, no. 1 (2007): 1-7, doi: 10.1080/15213260709336800.

2. Francesca Carpentier, "When Sex Is on the Air: Impression Formation After Exposure to Sexual Music," *Sexuality & Culture* 18, no. 4 (2014): 818-832, doi: 10.1007/s12119-014-9223-8.

3. Bradley Greenberg et al., "Portrayals of Overweight and Obese Individuals on Commercial Television," *American Journal of Public Health* 93, no. 8 (2003): 1342-1348, doi: 10.2105/AJPH.93.8.1342.

4. A. Rumble, T. Cash, and T. Nashville, "Beauty Versus Beast: Images of Good and Evil in Children's Animation Films," poster presented at the meeting of the *Society for Personality and Social Psychology* (2000), cited in Hugh Klein and Kenneth Shiffman, "Messages About Physical Attractiveness in Animated Cartoons," *Body Image* 3, (2006): 353-363, doi: 10.1016/j.bodyim.2006.08.001.

5. Sidney Jourard and Paul Secord, "Body-Cathexis and Personality," *British Journal of Psychology* 46, no. 2 (1955): 130-138, doi: 10.111/j.2044-8295.1955.tb00531.x.

6. Elissa Koff and Amy Benavage, "Breast Size Perception and Satisfaction, Body Image, and Psychological Functioning in Caucasian and Asian American College Women," *Sex Roles* 38, no. 7-8 (1998): 655-673, doi: 10.1023/A:108802928210.

7. Michael Levine and Kristen Harrison, "Media's Role in the Perpetuation and Prevention of Negative Body Image and Disordered Eating," in *Handbook of Eating Disorders and Obesity* (New York: Wiley, 2004), 695-717.

8. Sarah Murnen, Linda Smolak, J. Andrew Mills, and Lindsey Good. "Thin, Sexy Women and Strong, Muscular Men: Grade-School Children's Responses to Objectified Images of Women and Men," *Sex Roles* 49, no. 9-10 (2003): 427-437, doi: 10.1023/A.1025868320206.

9. Robert Goidel, Craig Freeman, and Steven Procopio, "The Impact of Television Viewing on Perceptions of Juvenile Crime," *Journal of Broadcasting & Electronic Media* 50, no. 1 (2006): 119-139, doi: 10.1207/s15506878jobem5001_7.

10. Pennsylvania State University, "Diagnosing 'Kind World Syndrome,' A Q&A With Mary Beth Oliver," *Penn State Donald P. Bellisario College of Communications*, accessed June 22, 2017, http://comm.psu.edu/news/article/diagnosing-kind-world-syndrome-a-qa-with-mary-beth-oliver.

11. Ibid.

12. Nicole Martins and Barbara Wilson, "Social Aggression on Television and Its Relationship to Children's Aggression in the Classroom," *Human Communication Research* 38, no. 1 (2012): 48-71, doi: 10.1111/j.1468-2958.2011.01417.x.

13. Sarah Coyne, "Effects of Viewing Relational Aggression on Television on Aggressive Behavior in Adolescents: A Three-Year Longitudinal Study," *Developmental Psychology* 52, no. 2 (2016): 284-295, 10.1037/dev0000068.

14. Sarah Coyne et al., "Pretty as a Princess: Longitudinal Effects of Engagement With Disney Princesses on Gender Stereotypes, Body Image, and Prosocial Behavior in Children," *Child Development* 87, no. 6 (2016): 1909-1925, doi: 10.1111/cdev.12569.

15. Amy Bleakley, Michael Hennessy, and Martin Fishbein, "A Model of Adolescents' Seeking of Sexual Content in Their Media Choices," *Journal of Sex Research* 48, no. 4 (2011): 309-315, doi: 1080/00224499.2010.497985.

16. Robert Cialdini, Raymond Reno, and Carl Kallgren, "A Focus Theory of Normative Conduct: Recycling the Concept of Norms to Reduce Littering in Public Places," *Journal of Personality and Social Psychology* 58, no. 6 (1990): 1015-1026, doi: 10.1177/01461672002610009.

17. Brian Borsari and Kate Carey, "Descriptive and Injunctive Norms in College Drinking: A Meta-Analytic Integration," *Journal of Studies on Alcohol* 64, no. 3 (2003): 331-341, www.ncbi.nlm.nih.gov/pmc/articles/PMC2431131/pdf/nihms53837.pdf.

18. Julia Buckner, "College Cannabis Use: The Unique Roles of Social Norms, Motives, and Expectancies," *Journal of Studies on Alcohol and Drugs* 74, no. 5 (2013): 720-726, doi: 10.15288/jsad.2013.74.720.

19. Solomon Asch, "Effects of Group Pressure Upon the Modification and Distortion of Judgments," *Documents of Gestalt Psychology*, edited by Mary Henle, (Berkley, CA: University of California Press, 1961), 222-236.

20. Albert Gunther et al., "Presumed Influence on Peer Norms: How Mass Media Indirectly Affect Adolescent Smoking," *Journal of Communication* 56, no. 1 (2006): 52-68, doi: 10.1111/j.1460-2466.2006.00002.x.

21. Dana Litt and Michelle Stock, "Adolescent Alcohol-Related Risk Cognitions: The Roles of Social Norms and Social Networking Sites," *Psychology of Addictive Behaviors* 25, no. 4 (2011): 708-713, doi: 10.1037/a0024226.

22. Gunther et al., "Presumed Influence on Peer Norms: How Mass Media Indirectly Affect Adolescent Smoking," 52-68.

23. For a review, see Shalom Fisch, "A Capacity Model of Children's Comprehension of Educational Content on Television," *Media Psychology* 2, no. 1 (2000): 63-91, doi: 10.1207/S1532785XMEP0201_4.

# 5 Media Parenting Strategy #1
## Alter Your Own Media Habits

So, now what do we do with all this information? How do we make sense of all this research? Based on everything we've discussed so far, we can say without hesitation or equivocation that media has an effect on children. But, if my conversations with concerned parents are any indication, it's not enough for parents to know that media has an effect. It's not enough to know why kids are affected by media. It's not enough to know what type of content is out there that we need to be worried about. Everything we've discussed so far is helpful and necessary. But what parents really want are strategies, research-based strategies that can help kids navigate the media maze.

We know a lot about media at this point. In fact, much of what we've covered probably isn't all that groundbreaking to many parents. So, if we know so much about media and the potentially negative effect it has on kids, why do today's children spend more time with media than any kids in the history of the world? If we know that media has the potential for negative effects, why are kids the most avid users of media? And what can we do to change that trend?

So, let's talk strategies. Media parenting strategies. You'll remember at the beginning of the book that I mentioned that when it comes to media, the group I'm worried about is parents, not kids. In order to change kids' media use and the way they are affected by media exposure, we shouldn't try to first change kids. That's how we've always tried to do it, and it doesn't work. Conventional wisdom won't cut it any longer. Our focus should first be, unconventionally, on parents. Research consistently shows that the best way to change kids' media use, and thus, how they are affected by media, is to change parents' media habits.

My home is probably different than your home. We have one TV. With rabbit ears, and no cable TV. I know, old school. Perhaps less old school, though, our TV hangs on the wall in our family room above the fireplace. I was lucky to even get it there—my wife wanted to put a painting in the same spot. Today, however, many homes have more than one

TV. In fact, 36% of children ages eight and younger have a TV in their bedroom.[1] On the surface, it makes sense that kids would watch TV more if they have access to more media devices, such as a television in their bedroom. Research, of course, supports this.[2] This is one reason why we have only one TV, and this is why we've put our only TV in a shared living space in our home. Research, however, has identified a host of additional factors that either predict or are related to children's media use. We won't exhaust this list of predictors, but what I will share is intended to help parents take the first step at helping shape their kids' media-related experiences by first changing themselves.

In a study led by Dr. Alexis Lauricella at Northwestern University, a nationally representative sample of more than 2,300 parents of children ages 0–8 responded to a slew of questions about their attitudes toward media, demographic information, and their own and their children's media use, all in effort to determine what factors help predict children's media use.[3] The strongest predictor of children's television use was *parents' screen time*. Parents' screen time, measured as the time parents spend with a variety of media devices, including TV, Internet, computers, tablets, smart phones, etc., unsurprisingly predicted children's time spent with these digital devices. The study also found that the more positive parents' attitudes are about various media devices, the more time their kids spend with those devices. Children's age was also a predictor of children's use of various media devices—older children tended to spend more time with media than younger children. Other research has found that keeping a television on in the home even when nobody is watching is related to greater television exposure for young children.[4] Interestingly, the time that mothers spend with media is a stronger predictor of children's media use than the time that fathers spend with media.[5] Children from relatively low socioeconomic backgrounds also tend to spend more time with media.[6] Other predictors of the time children spend with media include membership in a racial/ethnic minority group, children's BMI, and relatively little access to other things that create cognitive stimulation such as educational toys and parent-child reading time.[7]

You'll notice that some of these things can be changed with some effort on our part. I can't change the age of my children. And I can't change my racial/ethnic group. But I can alter other predictors of my kids' media use.

Let's keep talking about other predictors of children's media use. In a study involving 358 mothers of children ages 1–4, tablet use increased with children's age and with mother's tablet use.[8] In addition, children's tablet use was higher for children of mothers who had low levels of "relational well-being." In other words, when mothers were in a romantic relationship with a partner in which the quality of the relationship was poor, in which the quality of the parenting in that relationship was low, and in which conflict in the relationship was high, kids tended to spend more time with a tablet. Intuitively, these findings make a lot of sense. If a couple is fighting, if one of the partners is doing most of the parenting without much support from the other, and if the couple is constantly at each other's throats, those parents are going to be exhausted. They're going to have less patience with their children. They're going to have less time to spend with their kids because they spend so much energy on trying to keep a clear head. If that was me, I could see myself plopping my child on the couch and letting them play on the tablet while I made dinner, or picked up the family room, or closed the door to my bedroom and took a nap.

And since we're talking about the quality of marriage relationships, let me take a minute to share something about my wife. I never thought I'd say this, especially in public. I was taught to never say anything bad about my wife, but the situation demands that I do. The only bad thing I can report about my wife is that sometimes she makes me feel guilty because she's such a better person than me. Let me explain. Neither of us watch rated-R movies. After what we've learned in the previous chapters, I hope I don't have to defend myself too much on that one. But, not too long after we got married, my wife decided that she was no longer going to watch even PG-13 movies. If I recall correctly, we had just been to see *The Cider House Rules* in the theater, and we ended up leaving the movie because some of the content was too graphic for us. When she decided to go cold turkey on PG-13 movies, that meant I went cold turkey on them too. She was my movie-watching partner, and if she didn't see them, by default I also didn't see them out of a desire to support her in her decision. For several years, we kept this up until I couldn't handle it anymore. I don't remember which movie it was, but I remember that I just had to see a movie that happened to be rated PG-13, so I waited until she went out of town and I rented it from Redbox. Today, we're still evolving in decisions about what movies we'll watch. We no longer adhere to a strict no PG-13 rule, but before we see a movie, we often visit CommonSenseMedia.org to read the ratings and parent comments there. Every now and then, when my wife knows I want to watch a PG-13 movie, she sits and watches it with me simply because it means we get to spend time together. Bless her soul. After a recent such movie that we watched together, she turned to me and said, "I get to pick the next movie." She's a saint. Darn her, she's a saint, and that's the worst thing I can say about her.

If you were to ask my wife why she rarely has a desire to watch PG-13 movies, she'll give you two reasons. First, she doesn't like the way certain images, especially violence, stick in her head. PG-13 movies are rated that way because "some material may be inappropriate for pre-teenagers."[9] Recent PG-13 movies have been rated that way "for violence including intense sustained gun battles and fight scenes,"[10] and a host of other violent-related scenes. For example, *The Dark Knight* (2008) contained scenes of men being shot; a man being forcefully impaled with a pencil; a man hanging from a noose; a dog mauling; an image of exposed muscles, bones, and an entire eyeball; a bomb blowing up inside a person; and the sound of a man's bones breaking, to name a few.[11] Even one of the most recently successful PG-13 movies, *Wonder Woman*, contained fight scenes depicting arrows through the chest, gunshot wounds in a person's stomach, a man with a leg that had presumably been blown off, the gassing to death of a room full of men, and quite a bit of war-related killing. Which leads to the second reason my wife would provide for not watching PG-13 movies—if it's not okay for her kids (especially younger kids) to watch, why is it okay for her to watch? And if she does watch them, what message does that then send to her kids?

This amazing woman whom I somehow convinced to marry me understands that kids watch their parents, and that the example of a parent may be the most powerful influence in the life of a child. Research, not surprisingly, backs this up: there is a strong link between a parent's media habits and their children's media habits. Researchers at the University of Pennsylvania's Annenberg School for Communication, widely regarded as one of the premier media research groups in the world, surveyed a national sample of 1,550 parents with children ages 17 or younger.[12] Parents provided information about their own television viewing, their child's television viewing, and the number of televisions and other media devices in their home. On average, parents said they watch about 4 hours of TV every day. The average number of televisions in the home was 3, and about 70% of parents said they have a TV in their bedroom. In another separate nationally representative survey[13] of 1,786 parents of children ages 8–18, parents reported that they spend, on average, more than 9 hours (9:22) each day with screen media. More than 3 hours of that time is spent watching shows and movies on TV, DVDs, computers, smart phones, and tablets. Interestingly, the study reported that 78% of parents believe they set a good media example for their kids. Perhaps not surprisingly, the Penn/Annenberg study found a strong relationship between parents' TV viewing and children's TV viewing—this held true regardless of the child's age.[14] In fact, among about 16 different variables entered into the statistical model, the relationship between parents' TV viewing and children's TV viewing was three times stronger than any other potential predictor. Similar findings have been found in other studies (these studies are cited in the Penn/Annenberg study). In other words, research consistently shows that the more parents watch TV, the more their children watch TV.

The results of study after study suggest that if parents want to reduce the amount of time their children spend in front of the TV, a good first step is to quit watching as much TV themselves. Therefore, I offer Media Parenting Strategy #1:

## Media Parenting Strategy #1:
## Alter Your Own Media Habits

If we want to change our kids, we must first change ourselves. Coincidentally, the media actually teaches us this very lesson. Not that Michael Jackson was an expert on media parenting, or anything else for that matter, but the lyrics of his "Man in the Mirror" state:

> I'm starting with the man in the mirror
> I'm asking him to change his ways
> And no message could have been any clearer
> If you wanna make the world a better place
> Take a look at yourself, and then make a change.[15]

I think the message is true for dealing with kids and media. In order to change kids' media exposure, we shouldn't try to first change our kids' media habits. We should first try to change our own media habits. I think we might be surprised to find that our kids' media habits will follow suit. This is one of the reasons why I'm so adamant that we haven't lost a generation of children to the media. What we've lost is a generation of parents. And it's time to find them!

One of the goals I had in mind while writing this book is to alter parents' attitudes about media content, because I know that if I can change parents' attitudes about media content, then I might be able to change parents' use of that media content. Research and theorizing suggests that the more positive a person's attitudes are about certain media content, the more a person will seek out that type of content; and the more a person seeks out that type of content, the more positive their attitude about that content will be.[16] Let's put that more simply. I've talked about sports several times already. It's probably not a surprise that I am a self-proclaimed basketball nut. I still play regularly during the week. As I've mentioned, I especially love college basketball, to the point that the NCAA tournament in March is kind of like religion in our home. My wife grew up in ACC country—the home of Duke, North Carolina, and at one point, my wife's beloved Maryland Terrapins. Because I have such a positive view toward basketball, I am more likely to watch basketball on television, look at basketball scores online, watch highlights of the previous day's basketball games on espn.com, visit the sites of my favorite basketball teams, and talk about what I watched with friends who also enjoy basketball. Because I do all of these things, my attitude toward basketball will become even more positive, and the cycle continues. I like basketball, so I watch it more. I watch it more, so I like basketball more. And so on.

That said, if I can somehow help alter your attitude about violent media content, or about sexual media content, or about any type of media content—even if you began reading this book with a pretty strong negative attitude about these types of content—I will have accomplished one of the purposes of this book. Because, once your attitude is altered, it is likely that your media habits will change. And when your media habits change, so can the media habits of your children.

Changing our own media habits can be hard, especially when we enjoy certain types of media content. For example, in recent years, superhero movies seem to have grown in popularity. For a date night not too long ago, my wife and I went to the movie theater and saw one of these superhero movies. Right from the start of this movie, however, this particular movie kept getting more and more violent. At one point, a man was on fire and walked down a hallway, decapitating people with his fiery powers. Not wanting to be a hypocrite, and to practice what I preach, we got up and left the movie. Our kids later asked us why we left the movie early, and we had a good conversation with them about media content that is entertaining, media content that is worthwhile, and media content that contains little value. Kind of like the conversation we're having in this book right now. I wanted my kids to know that I was willing to make choices in order to protect my own well-being. It's my hope that if they know I can make these choices for myself, then the power is in them to make similar choices for themselves in the future.

Incidentally, around the same time as the date night I just described, I was involved in some research that looked at the effect of watching superhero movies. Led by Dr. Sarah Coyne, we surveyed parents of children ages three to six about their kids' exposure to superheroes on TV and in the movies, including common superheroes such as Spiderman, Batman, Captain America, and X-Men.[17] Parents also answered questions about their children's play behaviors. One year later, parents responded to the same questions. The study found that superhero exposure reported in the first survey predicted higher levels of male-stereotyped play (such as play fighting and wrestling) for boys, and playing with toy weapons (guns, swords, etc.) for both girls and boys, one year later. In other words, watching superhero movies is related to young children's behaviors that are similar to those portrayed in the movies.

I'm not saying that all superhero movies are bad. In fact, I took my daughter to see *Wonder Woman* because of the empowering messages it sends about women. What I am saying, though, is that when we understand how media exposure can affect us and our kids, we should critically analyze our own media exposure, knowing that our kids' media behaviors will likely mirror our own. This might mean that we have to choose different movies to bring home from Redbox or watch on Netflix. We might have to try turning the TV off a bit more in the evenings, and spend less time on YouTube or on social media. Ultimately, this means that the first thing we as parents need to do, in order to change our kids, is change ourselves.

My wife and I are at the age where we get invited to quite a few weddings and wedding receptions. While it's a fun way to spend a date night, I have always disliked the part of wedding receptions where guests write down or otherwise give marriage advice. I especially dislike the marriage advice stating that instead of trying to change your spouse, you should try to change yourself first. I hate that advice, but only because I know in nearly all cases, if not all cases, it's true. It is so much easier to hope that someone else will change. It's so much easier to hope that your situation will change, or that circumstances will suddenly turn to your favor. But nearly always, I think that the harder road, and the correct road, is to change oneself.

Let's illustrate this concept with another example. When my oldest daughter was a baby, we lived in a married student-housing complex while I was finishing a bachelor's degree. Our apartment was right across the walk from a playground where moms and little kids would congregate during the day. We developed a friendship with another family in the apartment complex. They had a daughter who was just a little older than ours. One day, the mom of this little girl shared a story with us that I'll never forget. Her daughter was in their house playing with dolls one day, babbling and mothering her doll like many little girls do. The mom was only half paying attention to the conversation between her daughter and the doll when she heard her daughter say to the doll, "I'm sick of your freaking crap!" Now, before we condemn this mom, let's take a step back and admit that that's pretty funny. There's no reason to mom-shame here because we all say things in front of our kids that they pick up, and that we regret. That little girl could only have learned that behavior from hearing it from her own mother. Imagine you were that mother, or that parent. We have two choices. We can scold the little girl and try to change her behavior. Or, we can place the blame where blame is due, and change the way we talk so that it reduces the chances of being mimicked in such as embarrassing way again.

So, let's talk a little about changing. There is a difference between changing our behaviors and changing who we are. I'm not sure which comes first. I think usually our behaviors will change when we change, but I think at other times we can change ourselves by consistently engaging in changed behavior. I think we can rewire our brains this way. To be a parent is to commit to a lifetime of self-induced change, something that can happen by changing our behaviors first. The media habits you had during college cannot be the same media habits you have today. Just as your metabolism won't allow you to eat the way you did as a teenager. Just as you can't stay up until the wee hours of the morning the way you used to. Just as you can't use the same language you used to, because now little ears are listening. Just as you put safety devices on cabinets. Just like you put the baby gate at the top of the stairs. Just like you finally gave in and started eating Fruity Pebbles with your kids. Just like you drive differently when your kids are in the car than you do when driving alone. Kids change everything, including parents. No, *especially* parents. The sooner we choose to change for our kids, the sooner our kids will start down the road of (1) not becoming what we once were, and (2) becoming the kind of person we hope they will become.

I'm convinced that big changes start with small changes. So, let's make the decision today to change our own media habits. I'm not talking about an entire overhaul of a way of life. What I'm talking about is to start by changing one thing here and one thing there. Here are a few things that we could do better in our homes—maybe they'll spark an idea or two about what small, unconventional changes you could make to your media habits:

- Play a game with a child before bed instead of watching the news.
- Turn the TV off during dinner. Start with just one day a week and see how it goes.

- Take one day a week and refrain from checking Facebook for the entire day. (If that sounds hard, maybe that's the perfect place to start!)
- Refrain from checking notifications on your phone between five p.m. and your kids' bedtime.
- Read to your child for five minutes before bed.
- Don't take your phone to your bedroom with you when you go to bed for the night.
- Watch educational TV (such as shows on PBS) a little more and cable TV a little less. (PBS is a nonprofit corporation, meaning its mission to educate makes its content different than most content found on TV today.)
- Make a concerted effort to look at your child, not your phone, when you're having a conversation with them.
- Keep the TV off for one evening each week.
- Choose the innocent movie at the theater for date night once in a while.

Two quotes sum up the message I'm trying to communicate here. The first is attributed to Confucius: "To put the world in order, we must first put the nation in order; to put the nation in order, we must put the family in order; to put the family in order, we must cultivate our personal life; and to cultivate our personal life, we must first set our hearts straight."[18] And the next quote is sometimes, and sometimes not, attributed to Mahatma Gandhi. Most likely it is a bumper sticker version of some sentiments Gandhi expressed. Regardless, it goes something like this: "You must be the change you wish to see in the world."[19]

If we want to change our children, and how they are influenced by the media, we must first change ourselves and our own media habits.

## Conclusion

One evening not too long ago around eight p.m., I walked into my family room, with my phone in my hand, and noticed that five out of the six people in my family were using some sort of digital media device. The only person in our family who was device-free happened to be asleep in her bed at the time. Now, we had spent the day with friends, running around outside, jumping rope, playing cornhole, and grilling burgers. Device time must be our way of settling down for the night. But as we've discussed, if it seems like our kids are always on their mobile device, the reason could be that they are simply doing what they see us do. Research from Common Sense Media found that 27% of parents feel addicted to their mobile devices, and 28% of teens feel that their parents are addicted to their mobile device.[20] In other words, if this is true, the lives of more than a quarter of American families are likely affected in some way because the *parents* are glued to their mobile device. And this doesn't say anything about how many parents don't realize that they actually might be addicted to their phone.

We spend so much time worrying about our children's media use—and rightfully so. It's been my experience, however, that things that I want to change about my kids' behavior are often things that I need to change first with my own behavior. If I think my kids need to eat more vegetables, it's painful, but that usually means that I need to start eating more vegetables. I hate vegetables. Especially green ones. Similarly, if I want to keep my kids from watching R-rated movies, then I need to avoid them. Kids learn from watching, and they watch nobody more than they watch parents.

This lesson was reinforced to me in a striking way not too long ago. I use the word "striking" because it took an actual lightning strike to learn something about changing my own media habits. Where we live, it's very dry. When it does rain, we don't get a steady rain. We get storms. Storms that swoop in and dump what feels like the ocean on us and then leave as quickly as they came. One night we were all asleep in our beds when we were awakened by a violently loud crash of thunder. I bolted upright, and before I knew it, all of the smoke detectors in our house were blaring. I jumped out of bed to check things out and found that much of the electricity in our house was not working. Using the light from my phone, I checked the breaker box and saw that many of the breakers had been tripped. I'm pretty sure lightning had struck our house. After the beating of our hearts slowed, we settled back into bed for what became a stormy night of fitful sleep. When we awoke in the morning, we discovered that the lightning strike had sent a surge of electricity into several of our electronics, frying them, including our Wi-Fi router. That's right, lightning literally blew up our Internet service that night. But the bigger blow occurred when upon discovering that our Internet wasn't working, one of our daughters exclaimed, "Yay! Less time on the tablet and phone, and more time together!"

And then I felt parenting guilt. I hate parenting guilt. I'll bet this story might be adding to your parenting guilt. But that's not my intent. I'm only suggesting that the way we try to get our kids off their phones or away from the TV or video games should change. Instead of the conventional way—lecturing them, grounding them, or taking away privileges because they use these devices so much—maybe we could start doing things a little more unconventionally by changing our own media habits and seeing how that works first. Hopefully it won't take a lightning strike, metaphorical or real, to get us to consider making some changes.

One last thought before we wrap up this chapter. Perhaps this will provide that last little bit of motivation to make one of the small changes that we're talking about. I think we as parents are pretty good at knowing what goes on in our homes. But for some things, I think we are blissfully unaware. Research involving children and media shows that there are some pretty big discrepancies related to media that parents *think* kids are consuming versus what kids are *actually* consuming. Research has shown that much of kids' media use is unsupervised by parents.[21] If parents don't know what their kids are doing online or with the TV, how can we know what we need to do to change? It shouldn't come as a surprise that parents often underestimate how much time their children spend with media.[22] And when parents are asked how involved they are with their kids' media experiences, again, it shouldn't be a surprise that parents report that they are much more involved than their children say they are.[23] What parent wants to report that they don't know what their kids are doing online? Getting honest reports from parents is tough. But if we believe child reports of how much time they spend with media, we can conclude that parents are largely unaware of their children's media activities.

Look, I get it. I'm a parent too. We're busy. We wake up in the morning and try to get ready for the day while trying to get other little humans ready for the day at the same time. We make lunches, pour cereal, brush little teeth, help tie shoes, zip up jackets, and then we all run out the door together and make it to school and work just barely on time. We work all day, either at the office, on the jobsite, or at home. We cook, we clean, we play chauffeur. We worry about our kids' friends and who they're hanging out with. We worry about their health. We worry about their morals. We worry about their safety. At the end of the day, my wife and I often ask each other, "Is it the kids' bedtime yet?" We're tired. We're stressed. And when we think about the media, we often just want to turn it on to help keep our kids occupied. I get it. It's hard. I've said all this before. I'm not the perfect parent when it comes to media. But, now that we know more about kids' media use and the effect that the media has on them, doesn't it make sense that we, including myself, should be just a bit more vigilant about what messages are coming into our homes? I'm not suggesting that we need to restrict all TV. I'm not suggesting that we have to sit down and read stories with our kids all the time instead of letting them chill out in front of an inane TV show every now and then. What I am suggesting is that we make a small effort, here and there, to change our own media habits. If we don't make the effort, who will?

A great place to start when thinking about Media Parenting Strategy #1—altering our own media habits—is to simply start observing our kids' media habits. For one day, we might subtly observe what they do. Watching their media habits just might give us a glimpse into our own media habits. We might learn a bit more about ourselves by watching our kids. And when we know a little more about ourselves, we'll know what changes we can start to make to our own media habits.

## Notes

1.  Victoria Rideout, *Zero to Eight: Children's Media Use in America 2013* (San Francisco, CA: Common Sense Media, 2013), 1.

2.  Amy Jordan et al., "The Role of Television Access in the Viewing Time of US Adolescents," *Journal of Children and Media* 4, no. 4 (2010): 355-370, doi: 10.1080/17482798.2010.510004.

3.  Alexis Lauricella, Ellen Wartella, and Victoria Rideout, "Young Children's Screen Time: The Complex Role of Parent and Child Factors," *Journal of Applied Developmental Psychology* 36, (2015): 11-17, doi: 10.1016/j. appdev.2014.12.001.

4.  Matthew Lapierre, Jessica Piotrowski, and Deborah Linebarger, "Background Television in the Homes of US Children," *Pediatrics* 130, no. 5 (2012): 839-846, doi: 10.1542/peds.2011-2581.

5.  Russell Jago et al., "Parent and Child Screen-Viewing Time and Home Media Environment," *American Journal of Preventative Medicine* 43, no. 2 (2012): 150-158, doi: 10.1016/j.amepre.2012.04.012.

6.  Helena Duch et al., "Screen Time Use in Children Under 3 Years Old: A Systematic Review of Correlates," *International Journal of Behavioral Nutrition and Physical Activity* 10, no. 102 (2013): 1-10, doi: 10.1186/1479-5868-10-102.

7.  Ibid.

8.  Tiffany Pempek and Brandon McDaniel, "Young Children's Tablet Use and Associations With Maternal Well-Being," *Journal of Child and Family Studies* 25, no. 8 (2016): 2636-2647, doi: 10.1007/s10826-016-0413-x.

9.  Motion Picture Association of America, "Film Rating," *Motion Picture Association of America*, accessed June 22, 2017, http://www.mpaa.org/film-ratings/.

10. *The Expendables 3*, IMDb, accessed June 22, 2017, www.imdb.com/title/tt2333784/.

11. "Parents Guide for The Dark Knight," *IMDb*, accessed June 22, 2017, www.imdb.com/title/tt0468569/parentalguide?ref_=tt_stry_pg.

12. Amy Bleakley, Amy Jordan, and Michael Hennessy, "The Relationship Between Parents' and Children's Television Viewing," *Pediatrics* 132, (2013): e364-e371, doi: 10.1542/peds.2012-3415.

13. Alexis Lauricella et al., *The Common Sense Census: Plugged-In Parents of Tweens and Teens* (San Francisco, CA: Common Sense Media, 2016), 1-44. http://cmhd.northwestern.edu/wp-content/uploads/2017/04/common-sense-parent-census_whitepaper_new-for-web.pdf.

14. Bleakley, Jordan, and Hennessy, "The Relationship Between Parents' and Children's Television Viewing," e364-e371.

15. "Michael Jackson Lyrics: Man in the Mirror," *AZLyrics*, accessed June 22, 2017, http://www.azlyrics.com/lyrics/michaeljackson/maninthemirror.html.

16. Michael Slater, "Reinforcing Spirals Model: Conceptualizing the Relationship Between Media Content Exposure and the Development and Maintenance of Attitudes," *Media Psychology* 18, no. 3 (2014): 370-395, doi: 10.1080/15213269.2014.897236.

17. Sarah Coyne et al., "It's a Bird! It's a Plane! It's a Gender Stereotype!: Longitudinal Associations Between Superhero Viewing and Gender Stereotyped Play," *Sex Roles* 70, no. 9-10 (2014), 416-430, doi: 10.1007/s1199-014-0374-8.

18. Confucius, *IZQuotes*, accessed August 2, 2017, http://izquotes.com/quote/340727.

19. Brian Morton, "Falser Words Were Never Spoken, *NY Times,* August 29, 2011, www.nytimes.com/2011/08/30/opinion/falser-words-were-never-spoken.html.

20. Common Sense Media, "Dealing With Devices: The Parent-Teen Dynamic," accessed June 22, 2017, https://www.commonsensemedia.org/technology-addiction-concern-controversy-and-finding-balance-infographic.

21. Donald Roberts, Ulla Foehr, and Victoria Rideout, *Generation M: Media in the Lives of 8-18 Year-Olds* (Menlo Park, CA: Kaiser Family Foundation, 2005), 1-140.

22. Brigitte Vittrup et al., "Parental Perceptions of the Role of Media and Technology in Their Young Children's Lives," *Journal of Early Child Research* 14, no. 1 (2016): 43-54, doi: 10.1177/1476718X14523749.

23. Douglas Gentile et al., "Do You See What I See? Parent and Child Reports of Parental Media Monitoring," *Family Relations* 61, (2012): 470-487, doi: 10.1111/j.1741-3729.2012.00709.x.

# 6 Media Parenting Strategy #2
## Start Talking about Media, and Don't Stop

In our family, we made the conscious decision to not show any footage of the September 11th attacks to our children. We figured that we'd show it to them at some unspecific day in the future when we felt that our kids were "ready." On the 15th anniversary of that awful day, I turned to my wife and said, "I think it's time we talk to the older kids about September 11th." She looked at me like I was crazy and replied, "They already know." I then asked each of my four daughters in succession what they knew about September 11th. My then six-year-old chimed in and told me about a video that she watched in school about how the planes crashed into the buildings. My heart sunk to my feet. Telling my kids about that was *my* job. I didn't trust anybody else in the world to handle the job of explaining the horrors of the world to my children. I felt violated. I felt angry at the school system. But most of all, I felt angry at myself for being so oblivious to something that was so obvious. Here I am, preaching to parents that there is no way to protect our kids from things in the media that will stop our hearts, and I thought that I had the power to control my kids' exposure to one of the most significantly infamous days in American history. I had fallen into the trap that I warn parents about.

There is absolutely no way to keep our kids from seeing things in the media. We need to purge that thought from our consciousness. If it exists, they'll see it. I don't know how to say that any more clearly. And that brings us to the crux of this book. How do we empower our kids to deal with media content *when*, not *if*, they are exposed to it? This is the most common question I get asked by parents, and it is the most important question. Once my children are in the media maze—and all children are—how do I help them navigate their way through it?

You've heard the term "shoulder angel," right? You know the image. On one shoulder is an angel acting as the conscience, and on the other shoulder is a devil acting as temptation. They both whisper into the ear in order to convince a person to behave, or not, in certain ways. Here is the first lesson about talking to your kids—your shoulder angel whisperings cannot have any effect if you don't offer them in the first place.

## Media Parenting Strategy #2:
## Start Talking about Media, and Don't Stop

My first recollection of the shoulder angel is an old Donald Duck cartoon. He is lying in bed when his alarm goes off. The angel in him gets up, turns off the alarm and tries to shake Donald out of bed. Donald is supposed to get up and go to school, but the conflict between his shoulder devil and shoulder angel lead Donald through a series of events and decisions that result in him skipping school to go fishing, smoking a pipe, lighting his tail on fire, and getting sick. The shoulder devil and shoulder angel ultimately duke it out with their fists in an attempt to sway Donald to their way of thinking. The shoulder angel eventually wins and convinces Donald to go to school.

Talking to your kids about media works in a similar way. Our kids see things in the media that have the potential to change their thoughts and behaviors, so kids need to have an angel on the other shoulder helping them make sense of the media messages. The shoulder angel comes in the form of parent-child conversations about media. However, the phrase "parent-child conversations" is a pretty nebulous, general statement. So, let's get more specific.

Children and media scholars have identified several ways of talking to children, and each type of conversation has a different effect on kids. Some ways are more effective than others. Let me illustrate the first way—providing facts—or as we researchers call it, factual mediation. Most elementary schools today have a series of lessons on media literacy. They may teach kids how to identify the various parts of a website, how to determine the authorship of websites, how to decide if a website is credible, and what organization is behind the website. Other school-based media literacy programs try to help children become more critical media consumers by helping them break down the persuasive arguments found in advertising. They may help kids learn how advertisers try to get them to think that a product is exciting, attractive, and desirable. These programs also help children learn that not everything they see on TV is real. A meteorologist is not really standing in front of a map, but is really standing next to a green screen. The yellow first down line on a football game—which I think is one of the greatest media inventions, ever—is not really painted on the field.

Like media literacy programs, parents can also share facts about the media with their children. They can tell them that "normal" women don't look like women on TV. They can tell them that the e-mail from a Russian prince saying that he needs $3,000 in order to transfer $2 million dollars to a US account is not legit. Parents can tell kids that there really aren't dozens of singles in their area just waiting to meet them. I believe these kinds of conversations are important educational tools, but alone, research shows that the provision of just facts about media is not necessarily enough to change how children are influenced by the media.

Dr. Amy Nathanson is perhaps the world's leading expert on the academic subject of parental mediation. Parental mediation is a term that we scholar-nerds use to refer to any parent-child interactions about media. Dr. Nathanson's 2004 study about the provision of facts to children about media helped direct the trajectory of my career, and revolutionized how parents should approach talking about media with their children.[1] In her study, Dr. Nathanson showed children (ages 5–12) a 5-minute edited clip from an episode of a children's TV program showing three superhero wrestlers fighting against some bad guys. During the 5-minute episode, three 10-second pauses were inserted into the video, during which a female experimenter read a message to the children about the program. One-third of the kids in the study heard a message that provided facts about the program's production, such as "those people in the show are just actors playing a part." One-third of the kids heard a message expressing a negative opinion of the characters, such as "all of those people in the TV show are not cool." And about one-third of the kids didn't hear any message. After the experiment, each of the kids filled out a survey. The results were interesting for several reasons. First, the kids who received the fact-based message responded no differently than the kids who received no message on measures of positive attitudes toward the aggressive characters, aggressive attitudes, and perceived justification of the violence. In other words, providing facts to kids about television production techniques was no better than saying nothing at all (we'll address this in a bit, but the messages containing opinions were the most effective). In fact, among the 10- to 12-year-olds in the study who were considered light-viewers of television, those who heard the fact-based message actually had higher average scores on measures of liking of the violent characters and perceived justification of the violence. These differences were not what we call "statistically significant," meaning that the statistical analysis cannot show that these differences would be found about 95 times if the study was conducted 100 times, but the numbers were consistently different. Said differently, this study showed that messages that provide only facts tended to make children *more* vulnerable to the effect of just a 5-minute clip containing violence!

There are a few possible reasons why providing just facts not only doesn't help reduce children's vulnerability to media messages, but actually can make them more vulnerable. First, some scholars think that providing facts may simply direct children's attention to elements of the show that they may not otherwise have noticed or thought about. It's possible that increased attention to these details actually resulted in children paying more attention to the violent content in the clip, which ultimately resulted in them being more affected by the content. Facts don't do anything to change one's interpretation of a message. If someone told me that Justin Bieber styles his hair with mousse, I would likely look at his hair and decide on my own whether or not I like it. But, if somebody told me they don't like the way that mousse makes his hair look, I would have to look at his hair with that thought in mind. Again, the shoulder angel can only have an effect if the thought has already been shared.

So, if messages containing facts are less effective, what types of messages do work? Messages with opinions. In the same 2004 study by Dr. Nathanson, the messages containing negative opinions about the violent characters, without exception, reduced children's liking of the violent show and of the violent characters, as well as children's perceived justification of the violence, compared to children who received the fact-based message or no message at all.[2] And compared to the fact-based message, children who heard the message with opinions had less aggressive attitudes after watching the clip.

Let's put this into practice then. If you want to reduce your child's vulnerability to the mean way people talk to each other on TV, you should do more than tell them that people don't really act that way. You should tell your child that you don't like it when people treat others that way, and that you don't like that TV makes it seem like it's normal and right to be rude to someone if you disagree with them. If you don't want your child to post racy photos of themselves on social media sites, instead of telling your child that people might get the wrong idea about them from the photo, you should express that you don't like it when people portray themselves in sexual, racy ways on social media and that you don't think it's cool to post photos like that.

To be sure, these are subtle—yet important—differences in the way we can talk to our children about media. You might not think that the difference between a message with facts about media and a message with opinions about media are that significant, but you might reconsider when we talk about the two types of messages in the context of school-based media literacy programs. How would you feel if your child's school teachers were empowered by the state to teach your child what is and isn't appropriate media for them? To put it in an extreme context, how would you feel if teachers had the liberty to tell children that they think pornography is healthy for children? And how would you feel if your child came home from school one day and reported that their teacher said graphic violence is enjoyable and that they think that in some situations kids should behave in ways similar to violent TV characters? I know, that's a far-fetched example, but one that should make you a bit uncomfortable. In other words, for good reasons, our public school system is not allowed to tell children what media content is good and what is bad. I don't want government employees telling my child what is wrong and what is right. As their parent, that's *my* job! It is for this very reason that school-based media literacy programs are confined to sharing scientific facts and to developing strategies that encourage critical thinking about the media. They cannot, and should not imho—this is texting language for "in my humble opinion"—be allowed to, encourage children to think about content in certain ways. It is not their job to instill certain values in my children. For this reason, while school-based media literacy programs are good, our kids need the opinions that can only be expressed by parents. Opinions, not facts, tend to do a better job at changing children's approach to media.

But that puts the responsibility right back onto your shoulders and onto my shoulders. And speaking of shoulders, we need to shoulder the responsibility of becoming the shoulder angel for our children by telling them what is good and what is bad, what is right and what is wrong. This is not brainwashing. This is not an exercise in intolerance. It is called parenting. And parenting has always involved transmitting values from one generation to the next. I wouldn't believe anyone who tells me otherwise.

Now that we know that sharing opinions is an important part of the conversations we should have with our children about media, we should discuss something that should be obvious but needs to be stated anyway. There are two different types of opinions: those in favor (positive) and those against (negative). It stands to reason—and research supports the idea— that opinions in support of a media message are more likely to encourage children's adoption of the message, and opinions opposed to a media message are more likely to discourage children's adoption of the message. In other words, if you want your children to learn the moral message that a show contains, or to adopt as their own the thoughts expressed in a blog post, then the opinion that you share should support the media message.

And if you want your child to resist a media message, you should express an opinion opposed to that message. I know, this is not rocket science. But it is social science, and it applies to more than you'd think.

My wife and I probably spend more time with social media than we should. Every day, articles appear in our feed that are written by bloggers, work-from-home journalists, and even national pundits offering opinions on a variety of social and religious issues. You know the kind of article I'm talking about—they address same-sex marriage, racial discrimination, child and sex trafficking, faith, proper expressions of faith, immigration policies, political candidates, parenting, self-esteem, self-image . . . the list goes on. My wife and I talk about these issues, and these conversations often come up in front of our children. In essence, we are talking about media content, and our kids hear these conversations. It's possible that our daughters that are on social media have read some of these articles too, and they can better put our conversations into context. But more likely than not, these conversations seem likely to have an effect on my children's reactions to future media exposure related to these issues. I guess what I'm saying is that I believe it is important for children to hear their parents' thoughts on difficult issues. Little ears are always listening, and we need to be sure as parents that our kids do not overhear us sharing a positive opinion about media content that we don't think is appropriate for them. What we say now can help our kids reinterpret media messages they will encounter in the future.

Similarly, my wife and I sometimes see movies or read books before our children read them, and we talk about them with each other. One of our favorite movies in recent memory is *Macfarland, USA*. As a couple, we saw it in the theater, and our kids heard us talking about it the day after. Because of the positive opinions we expressed about the show, our kids wanted to see it. And I could tell they approached watching it with positive expectations, especially since they knew we approved of the movie. Remember that positive opinions expressed by parents tend to reinforce media content, leading to children's adoption of the messages in the content. Our kids loved *Macfarland, USA*, and I hope that in some way they've internalized the messages in the movie about hard work, breaking down racial stereotypes, and acceptance of different cultures.

Now, by no means will sharing your opinion work every time in every situation. I'm sure there are many parents reading this book, especially parents of teenagers, who have seen more than their fair share of eye rolls and sighs of disgust when they have the audacity to share their opinion with their children. In fact, if you were to do a Google search on a site such as GoogleScholar, you'd find research that supports everything I've mentioned about parent-child media-related conversations. But you'd also find some research showing that talking with kids about media can have the opposite effect. I know, this is totally contrary to everything I've just told you. But remember, we've already talked about one reason why media-related conversations can backfire—conversations sharing facts instead of opinions can sometimes have the opposite effect because they simply draw the child's attention to the negative content. And research shows that parents can do something else besides share their opinions about media content in order to have a better chance at helping.

Even though scholars have been studying the power of parents to alter the influence of media on children for years, it wasn't really until the 2010s that researchers began to really take into account an important part of children's development—autonomy. As you know, autonomy, or an increased desire for it, tends to increase as kids reach adolescence. They realize they have the ability to choose for themselves, and they don't like it when things get in the way of that freedom. They especially want freedom related to things that are closely associated with their identity, such as sexuality, ways to cope with interpersonal problems, and dating.[3] It makes sense, then, that parent-child interactions, in all areas of a child's life, should be done in a way that support a child's autonomy. In fact, research shows that parents can support children's autonomy by encouraging them, responding to their needs, providing rationale for rules, and acknowledging a child's perspective.[4, 5] It makes sense, then, that media conversations that support adolescents' autonomy have a better chance of being successful at altering media effects than other types of conversations. And that's exactly what research has found. Researchers in The Netherlands surveyed 499 adolescents ages 10–14 and found that "autonomy-supportive" media-related conversations were related to a decrease in both family conflict and youths' antisocial behavior (such as verbal and physical aggression), and to an increase in youths' prosocial behaviors (such as helping others).[6]

"Autonomy-supportive" conversations were defined as parent-child media-related conversations in which the parents expressed curiosity about how the child felt about media content, or when the parent encouraged the child to voice their own opinion about the content. Types of parent-child media-related conversations that did not have the same positive effects were conversations that made the child feel like the parent thinks the parent is right, that the parent's opinion is the only opinion that matters, and that the parent doesn't care about the child's opinion related to the subject. The researchers concluded, "Parents can talk endlessly about media content, but when they avoid a real discussion with their child, their efforts seem to be in vain."[7]

To put all this in practical terms, then, let's talk with our kids about media. Let's tell them what we think about media content. And let's do it in a way that makes the child feel valued.

Let's recap. So far, we've learned three important things: (1) parents should share their opinions about media content; (2) the direction of the opinion (in favor of or opposed to) should correspond to parents' desires related to media content; and (3) media-related conversations should not be controlling—instead, they should help children feel valued by supporting their growing sense of autonomy.

Another common concern of parents relates to *when* they should have these conversations with their children. Should parents talk to their kids about certain media content *before* they are exposed to it, or *after* they catch their kids watching it, listening to it, reading it, or otherwise consuming it? Do I talk to my kids about something I don't think they're ready for, or do I wait until I think they're ready for it, knowing that they will likely already have been exposed to certain content by then? For example, do I talk to my kids about pornography before they're exposed to it, or do I wait until after I check their smart phone's browser history to have the conversation?

When my wife was pregnant with our fourth daughter, our oldest daughter started asking questions. "Where do babies come from?" she asked. "From heaven," we answered. "But how do they get into the mom's tummy?" "Well, God puts it there." "But how?" "Well, when two people love each other they can make a baby together." "But how!?" It was at this point that we realized this wasn't a line of questioning that we could avoid answering by distracting her or by giving her an insufficient answer. A five-year-old might respond with, "Oh, okay." But not this eight-year-old. She needed to know, and she needed to know now. So, my wife made a circle with her thumb and pointer finger, as if making the "A-OK" sign, and used the pointer finger on her other hand to show how a boy part fits into a girl part. "That's how," she said. "Oh, okay," my daughter responded. And that was that. We hadn't even broken to her the news about Santa Claus yet. That seems to be the world we live in now—kids learn about sex before they learn about Santa. While we may not want to think about it, our children's well-being requires that we do. And a study I conducted sheds some light on this issue of the timing of these types of conversations.

The study involved two groups of children: ages 5–7 and 10–12.[8] Each child, regardless of age, watched a 6-minute clip from *SpongeBob*

*SquarePants* in which SpongeBob and his friend Patrick fight with each other because they don't agree on rules for personal hygiene. Each of the kids, again, regardless of age, were told that they shouldn't act like the characters in the show, that solving problems with violence and fighting was bad—basically, the message involved an experimenter sharing a negative opinion about the characters' behavior. Here's where the study changed for some participants. Some of the kids heard this message before they watched the clip, some heard it during a pause in the middle of the clip, and some heard it after they watched the clip. Then, all the kids were asked questions measuring their reactions to the show, including how much they liked the show, how much they liked the violent characters, and how much they thought other kids like the violent characters. Results showed that the timing of the message containing a negative opinion about the show mattered, and the effect of the message depended on the children's age. For younger children, hearing the message at any time was better than not hearing the message at all. But for older children, they liked the violent characters less and thought that others like the violent characters less when they heard the message *before* they watched the clip. In fact, older children who heard the message after they saw the clip actually thought that others liked the violent characters more than the older children who did not hear the message. In other words, it was worse for older kids to hear the message after they watched the clip than to not hear it at all! To say this all succinctly, older kids respond more positively to media messages when they hear a parent's negative opinion about the content *before* the show than when they hear the opinion after watching the show.

I think there are several possible reasons to explain why it is better to talk to older kids about TV content before they are exposed to it. One reason may have to do with kids' age. Older kids don't like being told what to do. When they hear that they shouldn't watch a show, they may want to watch it even more. This is a perfectly normal and natural part of growing up. As children approach adolescence, and during adolescence, they develop the desire to make decisions autonomously without any restrictions on their freedom to make the choice. By telling them after they watch the show that they shouldn't watch it again in the future, they feel like their freedom to choose is threatened, leading to more positive attitudes toward the content. On the other hand, when they hear a negative opinion about a show before they see it—and then are allowed to see it anyway— they do not experience the same feelings of freedom loss because they were allowed to see the show. The result is that the negative opinion is given a chance to sink in.

But here's a potential media-parenting problem with that scenario. This research seems to imply that parents should allow their kids to see certain media content, as long as they have a conversation about the content beforehand. This is not quite the case, though. This research actually implies that the child will be exposed to the content anyway. Do you see the subtle difference? Parents can set rules, unplug the TV, monitor their kids' phones, use tracking software, and be extremely proactive about not allowing their kids to see certain content. Research shows, however, that despite all these well-meaning efforts, kids will still be exposed to this content somehow. It might be at a friend's house. It might be in the library at school. It might be on the home computer when the parent is at the grocery store. Or it might be indirectly through a conversation with a friend about what they saw online last night. There really is no way to guarantee that your children will never be exposed to certain media content. But you can prepare them for when they do see the content through the conversations you have with them. If kids are going to be exposed to it anyway, isn't it better for them to have the tools to deal with it when that happens, rather than trying to extract the media content from their brains afterward?

So, practically speaking, what does this mean for us as parents? It means that we should talk to our kids about pornography early and often, rather than waiting to find the magazine under their mattress, or in modern terms, rather than waiting until you catch them putting their phone away really quickly when you enter their bedroom without warning. It means that before they go to a friend's house to watch a movie, parents should talk to their kids about the movie. This means that we need to have conversations about substance abuse before they are exposed to the thousands of alcohol advertisements to which they will most definitely be exposed. For example, when one of our daughters was ten years old, she was invited to a sleepover at a friend's house. She and her friends were excited about the sleepover and made plans to watch *The Fault in Our Stars*. I hadn't seen the movie, so I looked up the rating. PG-13. Then I read the description and review of the movie on CommonSenseMedia.com. Here's what we found: "The central relationship is beautiful and mature and does lead to a love scene, which is handled tastefully for teen audiences (a girl's naked back and boy's chest are seen). Language is rare but does include one use of "f--k," as well as words like "s--t" and "a--hole." The teen characters drink champagne together, and a key adult supporting character is a drunk who's nearly always sipping from something."[9]

This might be okay for teens, but not for our sensitive little ten-year-old. So, I told her what the show contains and explained our concerns. She understood our concerns, and she and her friends chose to watch *Hotel Transylvania* instead. This doesn't mean that she'll never see this type of content, but she knows what we think about it. Hopefully, as research suggests, our opinions will be able to help her reinterpret what she sees when she does see it. And she *will* see it.

This also means that parents today need to be media consumers themselves. How can we talk meaningfully with our children about certain media content if we are not familiar with the content ourselves? Now, I am not suggesting that you have to look at pornography if you want to talk to your child intelligently and authentically about pornography. I don't need to stick my arm in a shark tank to know that the shark's teeth are sharp. I am not advocating binge watching of violent television. I am suggesting that parents be aware of what movies, TV shows, websites, games, books, and social media sites are most popular among children today (or that they will be required to see or read for school). Before we allow our kids to read the next dystopian romance novel, perhaps we should read it ourselves so we can have the moral high ground and the knowledge that comes only from experience when we talk to our children. Perhaps we should at least read reviews of popular movies so we know what they're about. And perhaps we should join Instagram and Snapchat or any other new social media platforms that our children may decide to frequent. In essence, parents need to be more media literate than their children. We can't possibly have the effect we desire to have on our kids if we don't even know what to talk with them about in the first place. And we certainly can't expect our conversations to hold any weight with our children if they know more about media content than we do.

Sounds like a lot of work, doesn't it? Maybe you already don't want to be spending more time on Facebook. Maybe you've already sworn off certain types of movies and books. I am not suggesting that you spend more time with any media yourself. But I am suggesting that we as parents—myself included—spend our time with media more wisely. Maybe we should spend less time entertaining ourselves with media, and more time using media to learn about the challenges and messages our kids will encounter. Maybe we should spend less time sharing pictures of our kids with other people, and instead spend more time reading reviews of the video games our kids are begging us for. And then, let's start talking to our kids. Let's talk to our kids before the media talks to them. Let's talk to them before they hear it in a nasty joke in the locker room. Let's talk to them before they encounter an unlocked liquor cabinet at a friend's house. Let's talk to them before they start exploring their sexuality online. At the very least, our words should be in their heads to help them interpret what they come across. At the very least, the shoulder angel should be given a chance to have an effect.

On my blog, ChildrenAndMediaMan.com, I often talk about the importance of talking to our kids about tough topics. One day, I received a message from a parent that said she was convinced that she needed to have conversations with her kids about pornography, but she didn't know how. She wanted to know what that conversation looked like, especially with really young kids who don't yet understand the concept of sex. The parent felt a bit paralyzed with fear of the Internet due to the availability of content like pornography. I think her fears are common. I think many parents feel the same fears. To answer her, and you, let me tell you what We've done in our family. Our kids know they have body parts related to their biological sex. They know some kids have different body parts that are related to their own biological sex. So, for really young kids, like our first grader, we told her that we don't like anything that shows body parts that should be covered by a bathing suit. For young kids, that may be enough about the type of content we don't like. We probably don't need to get too specific, because what we've already told them covers a lot of what can be classified as pornography. We've then shared with our kids what we think they should do if they ever see that kind of content, including turning it off, walking away, and preferably, telling an adult.

As you know by now, I'm suggesting that despite popular beliefs, I think a crucial, initial step toward changing how children are affected by media exposure is not necessarily to take away their smart phone. It's not simply changing the channel. It's not advocating for government regulation of media content. And it's not necessarily installing monitoring software. Instead, research shows that if we want to change how media affects our kids, we need to start by sharing our informed opinions about the media with them. But before parents can do that, parents need to have a certain level of media literacy. How can we have an opinion about media content if we don't know how to critically analyze it ourselves? Research shows that if we want parents to start talking to their kids about media, one place to start is by raising the level of media literacy among parents.

At Texas Tech University, we conducted a study in which we surveyed 177 parents from all across the US.[10] We found that the parents who do talk to their kids and who set critical rules about media are parents who are the most media literate. In other words, media-literate parents tend to talk about media with their kids, while less media-literate parents do so significantly less. The study also found that parents with higher levels of media literacy have more positive attitudes toward talking to their kids and toward setting rules about media. That shouldn't be surprising. When parents know something about media and can look at it with a critical eye, of course they want to share what they know with their kids. My concern is not so much with parents like you who are reading this—you're already on the road to increased media literacy. I'm most concerned about parents who know they should be talking with their kids about media, but because they don't know enough about the media, they don't even know what to say to their children!

I don't have statistics on how many parents are "media literate." Quantifying media literacy is a tough thing to do, and I'm not sure we can ever arrive at the state of being totally media literate. But, the fact that so few parents actually have regular conversations with their kids about media, and that so few parents set even rudimentary rules about children's media use, tells me that American parents are largely media illiterate. We may be able to read and write. We might be able to pay our bills online and know how to find the latest gossip on our favorite celebrities. We might know how to play Minecraft like a cool parent. But this does not mean that we are media literate. Media literacy starts with knowing enough about what content the media contains and how it affects kids that we begin to look at media with a critical eye. We begin to question the motivations behind the content we watch. We question the credibility of information. We know when to change the channel because we know what the potential effects of certain content are. We know when we see good, positive media content. And we have a desire to help our kids to also become critical media consumers.

Do we have a media illiteracy problem in this country? Absolutely. Are our kids affected by media? Yes. Could raising the collective level of media literacy among parents help change this? You bet. You know that my mission is to get research about children and media into the hands of parents. And now you know why. I want to raise the level of media literacy among parents so that they will start having critical conversations with their kids about media.

All of this information may be making you feel overwhelmed and inadequate as a parent. You may be wondering how to put all of this into practice in your already hectic lives. So, I'd like to open our home to you and show you what my wife and I are doing to implement some of this knowledge. We're not perfect, and your family situation may be different than mine, but here are some things we do that might help spark ideas for media parenting strategies you can use in your home.

## Family Night

In our home, we have designated about 30 minutes on one night during the week as "family night." Out of 168 hours in a week, we feel like 30 minutes devoted wholly and completely to a "family night" is not too much to ask of ourselves as parents. Our kids have come to expect this time from us, and if for some reason we forget, they will call us out on it. During this time, we do several things, but the largest portion of the time includes two things: some sort of lesson, and dessert. Our family night is usually on a Sunday night, since that seems to work best for our family's schedule during the school year. So, on Sunday morning, my wife and I choose a topic that we think is current and relevant for all members of our family (unless we forget, then we choose a topic 5 minutes before family night starts), and topics that are things we know our kids will face when they leave our house every day.

For example, we recently talked about marriage with our kids. Marriage, and how it is defined by both society and by religious organizations, has been, and I expect will continue to be, a "hot" topic in our society, and subsequently, in the media. For about 20 minutes, we talked about the different messages about marriage that exist "out there" and shared our opinions about the different messages with our kids. We asked them what they thought about different definitions of marriage. We asked them where they had heard these different messages. We explained our viewpoints on marriage, and as is our right as parents, we did all this with the intent of instilling our values in our kids. I am intentionally *not* sharing with you what my viewpoint is on marriage—that is not what matters for this discussion, nor is it the purpose of this book. The point is, our kids have no doubt where we as parents stand on the various issues related to the definition of marriage. They know why we feel the way we do. They understand that we know that others don't share our thoughts, beliefs, and opinions related to marriage. They know where messages about marriage come from, and they know from what sources we think they should look for more information about the topic.

Every now and then—perhaps once a month—we ask one of the kids to lead the family night discussion. They often choose safer topics, such as goal-setting, being a friend to everyone, honesty. We hope that allowing them an opportunity to lead a discussion lets them feel like they can talk to us about *anything*. *Anything* can be found in the media, so we want them to be talking about it with us.

As I mentioned, family night almost always ends with dessert. We sometimes forget about dessert and have to scrounge the pantry for chocolate chips and peanut butter to mix up in a bowl, but we try to do something. On good nights, we have no-bake cookies or even brownies. Hopefully family night leaves a good taste—literally and figuratively—in our kids' mouths when they recall our discussions.

## Dinner Talk

Another way that our family finds time to talk about these difficult issues is over dinner. We have made it a priority in our family to have dinner together as much as possible. Sure, sometimes dance lessons and track meets get in the way, but we make it happen at least a couple of times during the week. Family dinnertime is unique in that media-related topics seem to emerge organically as we talk about our days. For example, when one of our daughters was in seventh grade, she decided that she wanted to try out for the middle school basketball team. I told her that when I was a kid, I used to get my homework done after school and then head right outside to play basketball, where I'd stay until dark. In high school, as I've mentioned, I would get up at 5:30 in the morning to go outside and just dribble the basketball. Luckily, we lived out in the country when I was a kid and couldn't bother any neighbors. My daughter, like me, committed to a regular schedule of practicing basketball. She said she wanted to make the team. Fast forward two weeks from my daughter's commitment to do whatever it took to make the basketball team, and she hadn't touched a ball in several days. So, at dinner one night I asked, "How is your commitment to make the basketball team going?" She said, "Not too well. But Harry Potter wasn't good at commitment either. He kept going back and forth about chasing hallows or horcruxes."

Who knew that a tween girl would get that message out of a Harry Potter book! I'm sure she was just using Harry Potter as an example to justify her lack of effort toward her commitment, but the fact that she made that connection was startling, and sort of brilliant, really. With all four kids at the dinner table hearing this conversation, I took the opportunity, not to lecture, but to have some fun while sharing a quick message about media. "You know Harry Potter isn't real, right?" I teased. That's all I said. The point was driven home. Her feelings weren't hurt. We all had a good laugh. And after dinner she asked me to go outside to shoot hoops with her.

## Big Kid Talks

For a period of time, we also implemented what my wife and I called "big kid talks" on Sunday nights after the younger kids went to bed. This was our chance to talk in more depth with our older kids about things both we and they worry about. For example, about once a month it seems I inevitably read an article online about a girl who was sent home from school for breaking the school's dress code. The girl and her mom post a picture online of what she wore that day. And inevitably, comments are shared about the fairness (or lack of fairness) of telling a girl that what she wears influences boys' thoughts. Again, I won't share my thoughts on the matter. I will share that our conversations during our big kid talks related to helping our girls feel good about who they are as a person. There is nothing we want more for our girls than for them to have a sense of self-worth. We try not to lecture too much (though our daughters would probably beg to differ). We do try to ask questions and help steer our girls into thinking about their own self-worth and how they best should express themselves.

During another big kid talk, we simply talked about what I call "socialization agents." That's a fancy word that scholars use to describe all the different things that influence how we interact with our social environments. Parents are perhaps the most important socialization agent. The other four that make up the "big five" socialization agents include churches, schools, communities, and media. So, we had a discussion about how kids these days hear messages about a single topic from all of these sources. Some of these sources are louder than others. Some are in line with the values we want to transmit to our children, and some are in direct opposition to those values. We simply want our kids to realize that they can choose what messages they listen to and latch onto. That was about the extent of our conversation. It was more a conversation about making good choices, but I think they have a better idea of how media messages can influence those choices now. Yes, it takes effort to have these discussions. We don't do them all the time. But I'm glad when we do.

## Informal Conversations

The examples I've shared about what we do in our family to discuss media messages with our kids are examples of formal settings we use to address these difficult topics. Formal settings have their time and place, but I'm convinced that the informal settings may be even more important. It sure makes sense that having these sorts of talks during the normal course of everyday life can be just as, if not more, effective. If my daughter brings something up on the drive home from dance class, it feels so much more natural and less forced to share my opinions. By working these conversations informally into our normal everyday interactions, it's possible that our kids don't realize that we are trying to teach them, meaning that the walls that they might otherwise put up when they know we're trying to teach them never come up. I think there is probably less resistance to informal talks than to the formal talks. There may be many parents who might find it extremely awkward to start one of the formal traditions I've mentioned. I get it. They're easier to implement when started early in kids' lives, so they come to expect it.

For example, one of my favorite TV shows ever is *The Middle*. The mom, Frankie Heck (played by Patricia Heaton), is a lower middle-class mom who is overworked and underpaid, and she is always coming up with ideas on how to bring her family closer together. The family always eats dinner while watching TV. One day, Frankie turns off the TV and demands that the family sit down together at the table so they can talk and get to know each other during dinner. The kids freak out. They think the parents are going to get a divorce because the family only sits down together when there is big news to share. When Frankie tries to get her kids to share a compliment about the person to their left, the teenage son says to the teenage daughter, "Your head is basically the right size for your body." Sometimes implementing such efforts in a formal setting is just not going to work with your family. But the informal talks can. It takes work and a conscious effort to talk with our kids without coming off as lecturing and nagging, but it's possible.

An overwhelming majority of the research shows that these types of discussions—whether formal or informal—can have a lasting impact on children, their media habits, and their responses to others' media habits. Let me share just two research examples. The first study was one we conducted at Texas Tech University that explored the effect of educational TV programming on the social skills of preschoolers.[11] I mentioned this study in a previous chapter, but let's get into the details of the study a bit more. You'll remember that preschoolers were given one of two DVDs—either a DVD containing ten episodes of *Daniel Tiger's Neighborhood*, or a DVD containing ten episodes of a nature documentary. Parents had the kids watch one episode from their assigned DVD each weekday for two weeks. Kids then met with researchers who had them participate in tasks measuring specific social skills. Results showed that kids who watched *Daniel Tiger's Neighborhood* exhibited higher levels of empathy, social self-efficacy, and the ability to recognize emotions—each an important social skill identified as necessary for school readiness. Here's the catch though. These effects only happened among those kids whose regular TV-watching experiences were frequently accompanied by parent-child conversations about media content. In other words, preschool kids only benefited from watching an educational show like *Daniel Tiger's Neighborhood* when parents regularly and consistently talked with them about what they see on TV.

Perhaps this is the case, we argued in the study, because these parent-child conversations have taught kids how to more effectively and efficiently process television content. Or, these parent-child conversations about TV may reflect a different type of parent-child relationship that somehow allows the child to benefit more from lessons about social skills found in educational TV. Whatever the reason, this research suggests that parent-child conversations are essential to children's learning from positive media content.[12]

Another study we conducted involved older kids and potentially negative media content. We asked college students how often during their middle and high school years they had conversations with their parents about pornography and the effects of exposure to pornography.[13] Results of the study showed that the more frequently parents and children talked about pornography during middle school and high school, the more likely they were as college students to have negative attitudes about pornography, and the less likely they were to view pornography. In other words, parents' efforts to have the hard conversations with their kids during the critical formative years can actually stick and have an effect on kids when they leave home and are more free to make media choices for themselves. What's more, the study found that the self-esteem of college students takes a hit when their sexual partner views pornography—except for those youth whose parents frequently had conversations with them about pornography. Said differently, one way to protect kids' self-esteem from the damaging effect that their potential future partner's pornography use has on it is to talk with them about the negative effects of pornography. Perhaps early and consistent conversations about pornography convey the message to youth that their romantic partner's use of pornography is not indicative of one's undesirability. In our report on the study, we concluded, "Talking to adolescents about the negative effects of pornography appears to build the resilience of emerging adults when they become involved in a relationship with somebody whose actions could otherwise damage their self-esteem. Thus, active mediation [talking to kids about media] appears to be a specific form of communication that enables adolescents and emerging adults to effectively navigate the complex interpersonal situations that may alter how they feel about themselves."[14]

If we're going to change how our kids are affected by media, we can't expect to let somebody else do the teaching. The teaching is up to us as parents. We have to start talking.

Before I conclude this chapter, I feel like we need to have a conversation about the news. In the last few years, it seems like the world has gone bonkers. ISIS bombings in Europe and the Middle East. Both police officers and unarmed citizens alike being shot. Hurricanes, tornadoes, and tsunamis. Not too long ago, I read a story about a preschool teacher who abused the kids in her care. If hearing and seeing news reports about these things is hard for us as adults to handle, imagine how hard it is for kids to handle. In fact, research has shown that exposure to news, especially news of violent things happening in the world, is related to increases in children's fear, worry, and anger. That shouldn't be surprising to you at this point. And from what we've learned in this chapter, talking to kids about these things should help reduce the children's negative emotional responses to disturbing news events. That is, in fact, what the research shows.[15]

I was once reading a parenting book and came across some advice that said "*over*protection can result in the *under*development of children by depriving them of opportunities to solve their own problems."[16] So, does this mean that I should let my kids see the scary stuff happening in the news? Or, do I do what the research says and let them see it but then be sure to talk to them about it? I've wrestled with this dichotomy. On the one hand, I really, truly believe that kids grow up too fast, and that there will be enough time in their lives to worry about bad things. I want them to stay kids as long as possible. I hate the thought of them growing up and leaving the house. I hate the thought of them spending their childhood worried or afraid because of what they see on TV. I want their childhood to be filled with running through the sprinklers, taking trips to the library, and eating popcorn while watching a movie as a family. I want my kids to be kids. On the other hand, I know what the research says. I want my kids to have a firm grasp on reality. I want them to know how to keep themselves safe when I'm not around. I want them to understand that, yes, bad things can happen to good people. But I also know what watching news reports of shootings and bombings would do to my kids. They'd have trouble falling asleep at night. And as long as I get to be their parent, I want to protect them from these things. I also understand, however, that no matter how much I try to protect their eyes from scary things, they're going to see them anyway, at school, online, or even through conversations with friends.

As I wrestled with what to do about this, I reached out to a few people to ask for their advice. My wife and I are privileged to be friends with Rebecca Lucero. She's a professionally licensed therapist, and a great mom, and although she says she doesn't have research to support her thoughts, she shared the following:

As a therapist, I think parents should filter as they see fit. Just like not all PG-13 movies are the same, all news stories aren't the same. If you feel the need to change the channel there might be something that you sense your child isn't ready for. I don't believe in shielding children from the world, but I also don't believe in shoving the world in their faces either. I agree that discussing what children are seeing is helpful. I think letting your children listen to adults talk about some world problems can teach children how to problem solve, show empathy, and participate in their community. The real world is scary, but I think it is important to teach children how to have hope and be optimistic despite the challenges in life. It is also important not to burden children with hardships they can do nothing about. Each child will react differently, so I think taking an individualized approach to how you introduce your child to the world will yield the best outcome.[17]

In other words, each child is different. Each child will be able to maturely handle exposure to some current events, while other current events will be troublesome. It seems like there is a balance that needs to be reached between letting your kids see reality and helping them maintain the innocence of childhood. I guess what I'm saying here is that because parents know their kids better than anyone else, they are the one with the power and responsibility to make these decisions for their children.

I'd like to end this chapter with a personal story. This is purely anecdotal, but it's true, and it might give you some hope and inspiration as you seek to improve your media parenting. In the summer of 2016, my in-laws took my family to Orlando, Florida, to visit the theme parks there. One morning, we found ourselves eating breakfast at Universal Studios. I was enjoying my bacon and the smiles on my kids' faces when a person in a SpongeBob SquarePants costume walked into the room. If you know anything about me by now, you can probably deduce that SpongeBob is not among my favorite television characters, to say it lightly. He's my academic nemesis. Because I've read research about SpongeBob, and have conducted some research on the show myself, it is very clear to my kids where I stand on the quality of SpongeBob. In no uncertain terms, I have shared my opinion about the character and the show with them. I can still see the looks on the faces of my kids when SpongeBob walked in the room that day. They were looks of "Dad, can you believe who just walked in? We know all about him. And this is so not cool." Because I had already had conversations with my children about SpongeBob, nothing needed to be said, because everything was said when I shared a glance with my children at the very moment we encountered our collectively despised media character.

By talking to our kids, we can prepare them to face the raunchy, violent, debasing, and otherwise inappropriate media messages and images that they will undoubtedly encounter. We can prepare them to get the most out of the good, educational, esteem-building content that can be found in the media. We can teach them to effectively navigate the media maze. By talking to them, we become the shoulder angel that they need in the moment that they need us.

## Conclusion

The most common question I receive from parents who are concerned about how the media might influence their children is, "What can I do as a parent?" The short answer is, "Talk to them." Talk to them frequently and consistently. Share your opinion. Don't leave any doubt about where you stand. Do it in a way that makes them feel valued, like their opinion matters. Talk to them in formal, family settings. Talk to them when you're driving in the car. Turn off the radio and talk to them. Turn off football on Sunday nights and talk to them. Talk to them about difficult subjects. They are going to hear about them anyway, so they might as well hear it from you. Bring up pornography and legislation about marriage and legalization of marijuana and depictions of sex and violence. Ask them what they think. Support their ability to make decisions about their own media use. Be the shoulder angel whose whispers will fill their mind at the moment of decision. Be the shoulder angel whose words have the power to reinterpret the messages streaming in through the walls of your own home. Parents can make a difference in the lives of their children. Your efforts to have these tough conversations can pay off as your kids struggle through the media maze, even if you don't see any changes in the short-term. Keep talking. Please keep talking.

Notes
1. Amy Nathanson, "Factual and Evaluative Approaches to Modifying Children's Responses to Violent Television," *Journal of Communication* 54, no. 2 (2004): 321-336, doi: 10.1111/j.1460-2466.2004.tb02631.x.
2. Ibid.

3. Patti Valkenburg et al., "Developing and Validating the Perceived Parental Media Mediation Scale: A Self-Determination Perspective," *Human Communication Research* 39, no. 4 (2013): 445-469, doi: 10.1111/hcre.12010.

4. Eric Rasmussen, "Theoretical Underpinnings of Reducing the Media's Negative Effect on Children: Person-Centered, Negative-Evaluative Mediation Within a Persuasion Framework," in *Communication Yearbook 37*, ed. Elisia Cohen (New York: Routledge, 2013), 379-406.

5. Natasha Lekes et al., "Parental Autonomy-Support, Intrinsic Life Goals, and Well-Being Among Adolescents in China and North America," *Journal of Youth and Adolescence* 39, no. 8 (2010): 858-869, doi: 10.1007/s10964-009-9451-7.

6. Valkenburg et al., "Developing and Validating the Perceived Parental Media Mediation Scale: A Self-Determination Perspective," 445-469.

7. Ibid., 461.

8. Eric Rasmussen, "Proactive vs. Reactive Media Mediation: Effects of Mediation's Timing on Children's Reactions to Popular Cartoon Violence," *Human Communication Research* 40, no. 3 (2014): 396-413.

9. *The Fault in Our Stars* movie review, *Common Sense Media*, accessed August 2, 2017, www.commonsensemedia.org/movie-reviews/the-fault-in-our-stars.

10. Eric Rasmussen, Shawna White, Andy King, and Steven Holiday, "Predicting Parental Mediation Behaviors: The Direct and Indirect Influence of Parents' Critical Thinking about Media and Attitudes about Parent-Child Interactions," *Journal of Media Literacy Education* 8, no. 2 (2016), 1-21, doi: 10.23860/JMLE-2016-08-02-01.

11. Eric Rasmussen et al., "Relation Between Active Mediation, Exposure to Daniel Tiger's Neighborhood, and US Preschoolers' Social and Emotional Development," *Journal of Children and Media* 10, no. 4 (2016): 443-461, doi: 10.1080/17482798.2016.1203806.

12. At the time the Daniel Tiger study was published in the summer of 2016, I published a post about it on my blog, ChildrenAndMediaMan.com. I also posted a link to my blog on Facebook. Prior to this post, none of my blog posts had even reached 1,000 views. This post, however, reached over 650,000 views within a matter of weeks. People in more than 100 countries read my post. Now, 650,000 over the course of two weeks is not Taylor Swift video-type viral, but it was my first real experience with something going somewhat viral due to social media. I've since wondered many times why this post, and not previous posts, was so popular, and I've come to the conclusion that it has to do with change. We don't like to be told that we're doing something wrong with our parenting. It feels so much better to be told that we're doing something right. So, when parents saw research showing that letting your child watch TV can help them, they shared it like a hot potato. A common comment on Facebook "shares" went something like, "Hey, I'm doing something right," or "Now I don't need to feel guilty about letting my child watch TV." My most recent post as I sit here typing this on my computer had a grand total of, wait for it, wait for it, 7 views. The post was about

research showing that kids who watch fast food advertising actually visit fast food restaurants more often. Why wasn't this shared like crazy on Facebook? Because parents would have to turn the TV off, or they would have to start talking with their child about food advertising. That takes effort. That is a blow to the ego. That is telling me that I'm doing something wrong as a parent and that children's obesity might actually be related somehow to the content I allow in my house and to the content that I avoid talking about with my children.

13. Eric Rasmussen, Rebecca Ortiz, and Shawna White, "Emerging Adults' Responses to Active Mediation of Pornography During Adolescence," *Journal of Children and Media* 9, no. 2 (2015): 163-164, doi: 10.1080/17482798.2014.997769.

14. Ibid., 170.

15. Moniek Buijzen, Juliette van der Molen, and Patricia Sondij, "Parental Mediation of Children's Emotional Responses to a Violent News Event," *Communication Research* 34, no. 2 (2007): 212-230, doi: 10.1177/0093650206298070.

16. Lynn Robbins, *Love Is a Choice: Making Your Marriage and Family Stronger* (Salt Lake City, UT: Deseret Book, 2015), 115; italics in original.

17. Rebecca Lucero, through personal correspondence with the author, May 2017.

# 7 Media Parenting Strategy #3
## Establish Media Rules the Right Way

One of the most popular TV shows of the 1990s was *The Simpsons*. America's first family. The world's greatest dad. And the best blue hair the world has ever known. I loved *The Simpsons*, but my mom did not. She hated the crude humor, the fart jokes, and the occasional swearing. Like a mom should. For me, however, farts will always be funny. Especially when they come from babies in the middle of Sunday school. There's nothing like a well-timed baby fart.[1] Anyway, *The Simpsons* was outlawed in our house. I felt like the only kid in middle school who wasn't allowed to watch it. Luckily for me, though, my Boy Scout leader loved *The Simpsons*.

My scout leader had a shop out behind his house where we'd work on all sorts of projects. In Oregon, where I grew up, the rain never stops during the winter, so for our campouts, we would often hunker down in the shop. We'd sweep up all the sawdust, put some wood scraps in the wood stove, and bring the TV in from the house. My scout leader loved *The Simpsons* so much that he recorded a bunch of episodes on VHS. After dinner on these overnight campouts, we'd put the tape in the VCR and spend the next several hours watching episode after episode of *The Simpsons*. One night I think we watched *The Simpsons* for eight hours straight. It was fantastic! I had the best of both worlds. *The Simpsons* were outlawed at home—so I obeyed, at home—but the show was encouraged by the other authority figure in my life. In other words, I found a way around my parents' rules about *The Simpsons*.

On August 28, 2016, the *New York Post* published an article called, "The Frightening Effects of Digital Heroin." According to the *Post*, the article has garnered millions of views and prompted hundreds of parents to write letters of concern. Since then, parents have called for the elimination of technology in schools, and have even threatened to pull kids out of schools that require technology use. If your kids use media, the article suggested, they will turn into violent, screen-hugging, psychotic junkies. Celebrities have even gotten on their media parenting advice soapboxes. For example, Mayim Bialik, the actress who plays the neurobiologist Amy

Farrah Fowler on *The Big Bang Theory*, wrote an article titled, "Why I refuse to get my kids smartphones." In it, she said, "My boys are always supervised when they have Internet access. Always. I don't need to 'trust' them, I need to protect them."[2]

And so I return to the point I made to start this book. Our default as parents when we see something from which we need to protect our kids is to set a rule. To try to control the situation by attempting to prevent the problem from ever occurring in the first place. It's natural. It's instinctual. We want to protect our kids. If we see a mean dog charging at our baby, we step in front of our baby. When we see our child reach their hand toward a hot stove, we jump into action to keep her from burning her hand. But if you've taken anything away from this book so far, I hope it's the knowledge that we *cannot* entirely shield our kids from media content. We might be able to delay the inevitable by withholding technology, but our culture is so media-driven that thinking we can protect our kids from media effects is like a goldfish parent thinking they can protect their kids from water. At this point, we don't have the option of jumping out of the media water. So, we need to deal with media in a way that is somewhat contrary to our nature. We need to deal with the media maze in unconventional ways.

Now, don't get me wrong. Of course, I think we need media rules in our homes. I think there are situations when we need to take media away from our kids. In some cases, doing so may be the only way we prevent our kids from disaster. But by and large, research shows that setting rules for kids, especially as they get older, is alone insufficient to prevent the media effects that we worry about. I've said it before, and I'll say it again. If we really want to protect our children, we need to quit focusing on trying to protect them, and start making efforts to *empower* them. That was the whole point of the previous chapter. But that does not mean that all rules are bad, because research also shows that the way rules are communicated to and implemented for children may be one of the keys to empowering kids to deal with the media content they will inevitably encounter. As we'll now discover, rules aren't necessarily bad, but it appears that the only way to make them effective as kids grow older is to establish them in a way that makes sense to kids.

When we talk about media rules, I like to start by talking about rules for adolescents, because the research suggests that rules tend to work well for young kids, but not so much for adolescents. The real-life Simpsons scenario I described above exemplifies a phenomenon that social scientists call "psychological reactance." Psychological reactance refers to the feelings that an individual experiences when they sense that their freedom to choose has been threatened. We have all experienced this feeling of reactance. This feeling activates in us a desire to restore the lost freedom to choose, and in many cases, that freedom restoration takes the form of doing the exact thing that was forbidden. These feelings of reactance tend to be especially pronounced during adolescence. This should make sense based on what we know already about autonomy. I'm guessing you're able to think back to when you were a teenager and remember some things you did just because you were told not to do them. I'll bet that there are some things that you don't want to share with your kids. I can certainly think of my share of behaviors I'd like to keep from little ears. But that was part of adolescence. Pushing boundaries and establishing identity.

When it comes to setting rules about media use, then, psychological reactance has some real, practical implications for parents of adolescents. When a teenager feels like rules about media use limit their ability to make their own choices—and we all know that adolescence is the developmental period when independence is often most strongly asserted—some research suggests that the rules can actually backfire and result in even more of the behavior. This is why watching *The Simpsons* felt so good to me. I was wresting back my right to watch what I wanted to watch. Research exists showing that setting rules—what researchers in this field call "restrictive mediation"—has resulted in negative outcomes such as increased sexual activity,[3] and more viewing of the restricted content with friends or when the parents are no longer hovering around.[4] Media rules have also resulted in negative attitudes toward parents[5] and increased feelings of fear and worry when children do come across disturbing news events.[6]

Let's share in some detail research about the boomerang effect that setting media rules for teenagers can have. We'll start with video game ratings. Europe, somewhat like the US, has a system for rating video game violence. In one study, 310 Dutch youth ages 7–17 saw different violence ratings for games and reported how much they wanted to play each game.[7] Results showed that the restrictive age labels (7+, 12+, 16+, 18+, etc.) made the games more attractive for all kids in the study, including kids as young as 7 years old. The authors of the study call this the forbidden fruit effect— this is just another name for this idea of psychological reactance. When you can't have it, you want it more. This reminds me of the time a few years ago when Hostess announced that they were stopping production of Twinkies. It had been years since I'd had a Twinkie, but when I heard the announcement, I made it a point to go to the store and buy a box of Twinkies. I don't even like Twinkies. Taking a bite of a Twinkie that day made me wonder why I ever liked them in the first place. It was the possibility that I wouldn't have the choice to go and buy a Twinkie anymore that made me want to go and buy a box.

Another study[8] asked 496 seventh and eight graders about their social media use and about rules that their parents set about Internet use.[9] Results confirmed that the more rules parents set about Internet use for adolescents, the more likely adolescents were to include strangers as friends, as well as to reveal personally identifiable information on social networking sites. The authors state: "While restrictive mediation [setting rules about media] may be favored by parents as it is straightforward and easy to implement, excessive restriction can also result in unintended consequences, especially when imposed on adolescents with increasing pursuits of autonomy."[10]

Rules about girls' media use have also been shown to be related to increases in sexual activity, if you can believe that. In a study involving 528 adolescents ages 12–17, researchers asked questions about participants' sexual attitudes, sexual behaviors, and how often their parents told them they were using the computer or TV for too long.[11] Results showed that the more rules about media that adolescent girls had, the more sexual experiences they reported.[12] The authors argued that due to reactance, girls may have been more inclined to seek out ways to watch forbidden TV content, which in turn made them more susceptible to start experimenting with sex despite their parents' disapproval.

Finally, another study involving college students found that rules about media use were related to less positive attitudes toward parents, more positive attitudes toward televised violence and sex, and more viewing of televised violence and sex with friends.[13, 14]

It seems pretty clear from these few examples that psychological reactance is to blame for the way teenagers respond to rules about media. The authors of each of these studies referred in some way to this phenomenon. For years, researchers thought that psychological reactance was the logical explanation for teenagers' reactions to media rules, but no study until 2015 actually provided the first real theoretical evidence that this was the case. Remember our discussions about the way theory can explain media effects? Theory can also explain why parents' rules about media for adolescents do or don't work. There is actually a way to measure psychological reactance, and surprisingly, no research until the one 2015 study measured it in order to definitively claim that psychological reactance may indeed be the culprit in many of these instances that I've shared. Some of us at Texas Tech, led by then-doctoral student Shawna White, surveyed nearly five hundred undergraduate students and found that, indeed, rules about teenagers' media use led to teenagers' perception that their freedom to choose was being threatened, which itself led to this uncomfortable state of wanting to restore that freedom, which led to efforts to restore that freedom, which ultimately led to "boomerang effects," or the very behavior that the rules were trying to prevent.[15] Kind of a long and convoluted way to show that reactance is indeed the psychological mechanism at work, but it's pretty cool nonetheless.

So, what does this mean for you and your family? Before I answer that question, let me share a bit more research related to the setting of rules about children's media use. You'll see that rule setting doesn't always result in negative effects, sometimes for teenagers, but mostly for younger kids. For example, one study found that media rules reduced adolescents' intention to engage in oral sex in response to exposure to sexual TV content.[16] Other research shows that media rules that restrict children's exposure to media content that contains risky health behaviors actually reduces the likelihood of children's engaging in those behaviors. For example, research found that media rules were related to less TV-induced aggression[17] and to a decreased likelihood of children experimenting with tobacco and alcohol.[18] When setting rules works, scholars have mainly guessed that rules make children believe that the content related to the rules is not worthy of their attention or that the rules make children think more negatively about TV in general.

So, yes, we have research showing that media rules are effective, and we have research showing that media rules can be counterproductive. So, now what? Can rules empower kids? The answer may lie in research showing that media rules need to be established in a certain way in order to be effective. Which leads us to Media Parenting Strategy #3:

## Media Parenting Strategy #3:
## Establish Media Rules the Right Way

Do you ever wish your kids would listen to you without them asking the oft-dreaded question, "Why?" Why do I have to put on pants? Why do I have to use silverware when my hands work just fine? Why do I have to shower when I'm just going to get dirty again? Despite the sometimes superhuman effort it takes to provide answers to all the "why" questions when you set a rule for your kids, research exists showing that providing reasons for the rules might make all the difference in determining whether or not rules have the desired effect. In the case of media parenting, the desired effect is for rules to empower—that's where the real protection comes. For example, the same study showing that parent-child media-related conversations need to be autonomy-supportive that we discussed in the last chapter also showed that, just like autonomy-supportive media-related conversations, autonomy-supportive rules setting about media is likewise related to increases in prosocial behavior, and to decreases in family conflict and antisocial behavior.[19] So just what is autonomy-supportive rule setting? To be short, it is rule setting accompanied by explanations for those rules. In another study, 1,029 adolescents ages 10–14 were surveyed about the rules parents set for them about media use.[20] The study found that rules about TV led to less media violence exposure and to decreased aggression among kids, but only when the rules were accompanied by questions or statements that helped explain the reasons for the rules. When rules were perceived as controlling or inconsistent, they didn't have the same positive effect. In other words, when kids understand the reasons why they aren't allowed to participate in some media activities, they seem to be more willing to adhere to the rules. On the other hand, when kids think their parents will get mad or threaten to punish them if they watch certain shows or movies, or play certain video games, the rules are less effective.

So, when we talk about media rules, setting rules by itself isn't enough. They don't empower. Alone they can even be counterproductive. It's not enough to take away their phone, or not get one for them in the first place. It's not enough to set limits on how much time kids can spend with TV, on the tablet, or using their phone. Practically, then, when we set rules about our kids' media use, explanations should always be given about those rules. Rules should be accompanied by explanations for why parents think kids shouldn't watch certain shows or movies or play certain games. This doesn't really sound like "unconventional" media parenting, does it? But if the conventional approach to media parenting is to default to rules, then the simple act of adding explanations to our rules may very well be the definition of unconventional media parenting.

One of our daughters is obsessed with Harry Potter, and I don't use the word "obsessed" lightly. She has read all seven books, from first to last, from last to first, and in no particular order. Just for fun, she's made lists of all the characters' names that she can remember. She's even tried to get away with things by saying, "But that's not what Harry would do," and, as I mentioned previously, "But Harry Potter wasn't good at commitment either." I've never seen a girl so excited to visit Diagon Alley at Universal Studios, try Butterbeer, or visit Ollivander's wand shop. I'm beginning to wonder if she might actually have been a witch in a previous life and now she's stuck with us lowly Muggle parents. Sometimes I wish I had magical powers so I could get her to clean her room. Before her thirteenth birthday, we let her watch all the Harry Potter movies, except the ones that are PG-13. She knows we have the PG-13 rule for kids twelve and under, but since she had read the books, she didn't see why she had to wait. If she'd already been exposed to the content in word format, what would be the difference if she saw it in video format, she argued. Until we gave her a reason why we had this rule. When she was younger, this daughter used to have trouble falling asleep at night. She often laid in bed and let her imagination about what could happen in the dark run wild in her mind. She has been kept awake by media content we thought was pretty innocuous. So, we explained about the killing (avada kedavra!), the monsters, fight scenes, (spoiler alert!) deaths of beloved red-haired characters, and the other graphic content in the Harry Potter movies that cause them to be rated PG-13. We told her we were concerned that until she was able to keep herself together after watching something that is somewhat intense, then, no, she couldn't watch them. She almost wholeheartedly agreed that this was a smart choice, apparently realizing that she didn't want to voluntarily trigger insomnia.

In other words, kids want to understand why. They ask "why" for a very legitimate reason. They want an explanation that makes sense to them and that serves their self-interests. "Because" is not a good enough reason. Neither is its extension, "Because I said so." You were the same way as a child, and you are probably that way with a lot of things now. Kids need an explanation for media rules that makes sense to them. I think when kids understand the reasons why parents set media rules for them, they are more likely to buy into the rules themselves, and thus, better abide by them. And by the way, our daughter has since watched all the Harry Potter movies without them disrupting her sleep. So, parents of young children, take hope in the fact that kids grow out of some things. If they only grew out of costing us money.

The explanations we offer for the media rules we set should be stated in a way that allows children to feel like the parent has confidence in their ability to make good choices about media choices. In other words, kids want to know that we trust them. And when we've done all we can as a parent to set appropriate rules, and to explain those rules the best we can, what more can we do besides trust our kids to make good decisions?

Now, despite research, I'm convinced that each child is different. I don't need research to tell me this. I can look at my own family and come to this conclusion. Because each child is different, it's possible that children, even in the same family, may respond to rules and their accompanying explanations differently. One of our daughters came out of the womb as a responsible adult in many respects. She's not really into technology. Texting is kind of an annoyance to her. She's a homebody. On most Friday nights, she's content to hang out at home, babysit for us or for another family, or rent a movie and crash in the family room. She has her own phone and pays for her monthly service herself, but she doesn't spend enough time on it to cause us any concern. Another daughter, on the other hand, is one of those stereotypical tech-junkie teenage girls. She's the one I mentioned at the start of this book. When she's doing homework, she has music playing on her phone. She watches TV at the same time she watches videos on her phone. I'm sure we're not the only family with such different children. With any of the studies I've cited about media rule setting, the results could have been completely different if parents answered survey questions with a different child in mind. Perhaps this is another reason why some studies show that rules work and why others suggest that rules backfire. The rules that work for one child may not, and likely will not, work the same for another child, even in the same family. Parents know their children best. Parents know the tendencies, weaknesses, interests, and potential typical reactions of their children. So, my best recommendation about media rule setting, in addition to what we've already discussed about providing explanations for the rules, is to start making what you think are child-specific rules for your child at a young age, and to remain flexible as your child grows.

You may be sitting there thinking, "How does this help me decide whether or not to let my daughter download the Instagram app?" "How am I supposed to know when she's ready for a smart phone, Snapchat, or a Facebook account?" "Some help you are, Rasmussen." These are fair thoughts to have. For example, when our daughter turned thirteen, we let her get her own Facebook account. She announced her newfound identity to all of our relatives. My sister, who also has teenage kids, somewhat jokingly responded, "Don't tell your cousins that you have a Facebook account, because I still won't let them have one."

Every family is different. But, I think there are some rules that seem appropriate for all kids, despite their differences. And don't forget that with all these rules, we try to provide explanations as best we can. Hopefully, these ideas will spark a thought or two about how to set rules about the media for your unique kids. So, just in case it helps, here are some of the general media rules in our home.

- No phones in the bedroom at or after bedtime. This rule goes for me and my wife as well.
- No TVs in the bedroom, including the master bedroom. As an aside, this rule actually serves a dual purpose for my wife and me.

I once read a study that said couples with a TV in the bedroom have sex less often. Boom, decision made.

- No Facebook until my kids are thirteen, and when they do get on Facebook, Mom or Dad get to know the passwords and can access the account at any time.
- We are friends with our kids on social media, such as Facebook.
- No PG-13 movies until my kids are thirteen. While I realize that is an arbitrary age that was developed by industry-types, we feel like there is little in PG-13 movies that is worth our children watching anyway. When our kids do turn thirteen, we usually see the movie before they watch it. Now, even though I say this is a hard rule, we did allow our daughter to watch *Star Wars Episode VII* before she turned thirteen. I saw it and knew she would love it, and I don't recall seeing much that I thought would influence her well-being in a negative way. Sure, there is shooting, fighting, and death, but something in me told me that taking her to the movie would do more for her than not seeing the movie. Watching it together was a great daddy-daughter night out. That night is a good memory for both of us. Rules are rules, and sometimes rules can be broken if the situation permits, but our kids know generally where we stand on movie rules.
- We don't have a video game console, and lucky for us, our kids have never expressed any real interest in video games beyond the free ones they can download on the tablet. I don't think video games are inherently bad. If we had a game console, we'd be picky about the games we'd allow our kids to play, and we'd likely limit them to problem-solving or sports-related games.
- And finally, we do not allow Instagram, Snapchat, or other photo-sharing social media. I was a teenage boy once. I know how boys think. I can only imagine what boys do, and want girls to do for them, on photo-sharing social media. Research also says something about boys, girls, and sexting—be sure to read about it in the Appendix.

And that's about it for the media rules we set in our home. What these rules do is allow us to almost always be aware of the media content to which our children are exposed. Sure, they probably watch and listen to things that they we'd prefer they didn't. Yes, they probably spend more time with media than they should. And it's possible that they see things and visit sites and do things with media that we don't know about. But I feel like these rules, coupled with explanations for them, have a greater potential to empower my kids to deal with undesirable media content than rules that are perceived by kids as a way to control them.

Setting rules and providing explanations and then letting go by letting our kids make their own media decisions seems risky, doesn't it? Mayim Bialik was right on that point. We are supposed to protect our kids, and not just trust them to make good decisions, right? But when we change our perspective from protecting our kids to empowering them, things change. Are our kids going to make some bad decisions about media? Of course. They'll likely make bad decisions in other aspects of their lives too. And we'll have to then provide consequences, like taking their phone away. It's bound to happen, both the mistakes and the consequences. I know it's hard to accept, but just like we have done some stupid things, our kids will also do some stupid things. But that's not the end of the world. We all make mistakes. We all do things of which we are not proud. No number of rules or talking will prevent all mistakes. But, I think setting rules in the right way can help minimize the mistakes, because it can empower our kids. In fact, giving our children enough leash to make mistakes and learn from those mistakes through natural or imposed consequences is perhaps one of the most powerful things we can do as parents.

It's not just research that has taught me this. I've learned this through some very personal experiences in our family. In fact, it is in this regard that I think my wife and I share one of our biggest parenting regrets. One of our kids has an intense fear of making mistakes. If she forgets to do a chore, she beats herself up. If she gets less than a perfect score on a school assignment, she feels guilty. If she burns a piece of toast, she feels bad for wasting bread. Is this a personality fault of her own? Absolutely not. I believe that early in her life, we were hard on her for some reason. I'd like to think it was related to our inexperience as parents, but it probably says something about our own mental make-up.

Whatever the reason, we didn't allow her to make many mistakes. We probably parented in a way that made her feel shame for not meeting expectations. If I could go back to her as a three- or five-year-old, I would tell her over and over again that it's okay to make mistakes. That we love her no matter how successful she is in the ways that society measures success. I would laugh more at the silly things. I would lay down expectations and then take an attitude more consistent with the attitude of Crush, the turtle from *Finding Nemo*. I'd "kill the motor, dude. Let us see what Squirt does flying solo." I would tell her, "You so totally rock, Squirt! So gimme some fin." When Marlin asked Crush how he could know if kids are ready to try something on their own, Crush said, "Well, you never really know, but when they know, you know, y'know?"

I look at my daughter now and look at the rules I set and the mistakes I didn't let her make. Instead of allowing rules to parent, *I* needed to be the one to parent. My daughter needs to know that I trust her. That I believe in her. And that I have confidence in her ability to make decisions on her own. She needs to know that I think she is amazing. That I think she's responsible. That I'm amazed at her maturity, her compassion, her desire to do what's right and be a good person. She needs to know that I pray that she'll forgive me for putting too much pressure on her. She needs to know that she is valuable. That she's worth it. That she's extraordinary. That I admire her. That I wish I could be more like her. That she doesn't need to beat herself up, because she has nothing to be forgiven of. That she can just be herself. That her best is good enough. That it always has been and always will be. And the same goes for each of my daughters.

Media parenting by rules alone is default media parenting. It's conventional media parenting. I don't want to be a default parent anymore. I don't want to be a conventional parent. I want to be an unconventional, extraordinary parent. I want to show my kids that I respect them by helping them understand what I know about media. When they understand it for themselves, the rules will make better sense. They'll have a better chance of sticking, and ultimately, helping them through the media maze.

**Conclusion**

To end this chapter, let's talk about some research that combines several things we've discussed, because something extraordinary happens when we look at things with both talking and setting rules in mind. First, recall what we know about norms from the chapter on how media exposure affects kids—when we think others are doing something, we're also more likely to do it. Norms also work in another way. When we think that others *think* we should act a certain way, we're more likely to act that way. For example, if I think my boss thinks I should be in my office until five p.m. every day, I'm more likely to stick around until five every day. Now recall the research we talked about showing that parent-child conversations about pornography in middle school and high school can help prevent kids from seeking out pornography when they go to college. Now, consider a study I was a part of that combines the influence of norms and parent-child interactions about pornography. [21] We had college students sit at a computer and answer a bunch of questions about various behaviors such as littering, doing homework, going to church, drinking alcohol, volunteering, and yes, viewing pornography. As fast as they could, participants had to push a button corresponding with "yes" or "no" when asked if certain people in their lives would want them to do those activities. Among all these questions, participants saw a question asking if their parents would want them to look at pornography. A faster "no" response is indicative of greater "norm accessibility." In other words, we wanted to see how top of mind parents' beliefs about pornography use were in the mind of college students. We found that rules about pornography during middle school and high school were related to greater norm accessibility—the thought that parents disapprove of pornography use—and these thoughts were, in turn, related to less pornography use as a college student. So, when kids went to college and had the choice to look at pornography, their parents' rules, and what those rules communicated, came to mind. While these results are cool, I don't think they're complete. I think the rules did in fact communicate parents' disapproval of viewing pornography to these students. But, we need to look at this study in combination with the previous study showing that it was parent-child conversations that prevented future pornography use. Taken together, the findings are striking—it's the combination of talking to kids *and* setting rules about media content that helps prevent kids from choosing to view that content in the future.

Rules communicate disapproval. But words explain why. The combination of the two produces results. Kind of like peanut butter and chocolate. Peanut butter is good. Chocolate is good. But when you put them together, something amazing happens.

Notes

1. Remember in one of the *Despicable Me* movies that one of Gru's secret weapons was a fart gun? I have a replica in my office that makes real fart noises. It comes in handy when I have a stubborn student in my office.

2. Mayim Bialik, "Mayim Bialik: Why I Refuse to Get My Kids Smartphones," *Kveller*, August 25, 2016, www.kveller.com/mayim-bialik-why-i-refuse-to-get-my-kids-smartphones/.

3. Peter Nikken and Hanneke de Graaf, "Reciprocal Relationships Between Friends' and Parental Mediation of Adolescents' Media Use and Their Sexual Attitudes and Behavior," *Journal of Youth and Adolescence* 42, no. 11 (2013): 1696-1707, doi: 10.1007/s10964-012-9873-5.

4. Amy Nathanson, "The Unintended Effects of Parental Mediation of Television on Adolescents," *Media Psychology* 4, no. 3 (2002): 207-230, doi: 10.1207/S1532785XMEP0403_01.

5. Ibid.

6. Moniek Buijzen, Juliette van der Molen, and Patricia Sondij, "Parental Mediation of Children's Emotional Responses to a Violent News Event," *Communication Research* 34, no. 2 (2007): 212-230, doi: 10.1177/0093650206298070.

7. Marije Bijvank et al., "Age and Violent-Content Labels Make Video Games Forbidden Fruits for Youth." *Pediatrics* 123, no. 3 (2009): 870-876, doi: 10.1542/peds.2008-0601.

8. Wonsun Shin and Nurzali Ismail, "Exploring the Role of Parents and Peers in Young Adolescents' Risk Taking on Social Networking Sites," *Cyberpsychology, Behavior, and Social Networking* 17, no. 9 (2014): 578-583, doi: 10.1089/cyber.2014.0095.

9. Questions related to how often parents determine which websites that kids can or cannot visit, as well as other ways that parents control or restrict kids' Internet use. The survey also asked kids about their risky social networking behavior, including whether or not they had ever added someone as a friend whom they had never met face-to-face, what their privacy settings were for their social networking sites, and what types of information they allowed anybody to see.

10. Shin and Ismail, "Exploring the Role of Parents and Peers in Young Adolescents' Risk Taking on Social Networking Sites," 582.

11. Nikken and de Graaf, "Reciprocal Relationships Between Friends' and Parental Mediation of Adolescents' Media Use and Their Sexual Attitudes and Behavior."

12. Measured as the most intimate sexual behavior they had ever engaged in, ranked from less intimate to most intimate: dating, deep kissing, light petting, heavy petting, and sexual intercourse.

13. Nathanson, "The Unintended Effects of Parental Mediation of Television on Adolescents," 207-230.

14. Students were asked to think back to their high school years as they responded to a survey asking about media rules, exposure to certain content, and attitudes toward the content and toward their parents.

15. Shawna White, Eric Rasmussen, and Andy King, "Restrictive Mediation and Unintended Effects: Serial Multiple Mediation Analysis Explaining the Role of Reactance in U.S. Adolescents," *Journal of Children and Media* 9, no. 4 (2015), 510-527, doi: 10.1080/17482798.2015.1088873.

16. Deborah Fisher et al., "Televised Sexual Content and Parental Mediation: Influences on Adolescent Sexuality," *Media Psychology* 12, no. 2 (2009): 121-147, doi: 10.1080/15213260902849901.

17. Amy Nathanson, "Identifying and Explaining the Relationship between Parental Mediation and Children's Aggression," *Communication Research* 26, no. 2 (1999): 124-143, doi: 10.1177/009365099026002002.

18. Susanne Tanski et al., "Parental R-Rated Movie Restriction and Early-Onset Alcohol Use," *Journal of Studies on Alcohol and Drugs* 71, no. 3 (2010): 452-459, www.ncbi.nlm.nih.gov/pmc/articles/PMC2859793/pdf/jsad452.pdf.

19. Patti Valkenburg et al., "Developing and Validating the Perceived Parental Media Mediation Scale: A Self-Determination Perspective," *Human Communication Research* 39, no. 4 (2013): 445-469, doi: 10.1111/hcre.12010.

20. Karin Fikkers, Jessica Piotrowski, and Patti Valkenburg, "A Matter of Style? Exploring the Effects of Parental Mediation Styles on Early Adolescents' Media Violence Exposure and Aggression," *Computers in Human Behavior* 70, (2017): 407-415, doi: 10.1016/j.chb.2017.01.029.

21. Eric Rasmussen et al., "The Relation Between Norm Accessibility, Pornography Use, and Parental Mediation Among Emerging Adults," *Media Psychology* 19, no. 3 (2016): 431-454, doi: 10.1080/15213269.2015.1054944.

# 8 Media Parenting Strategy #4
## Participate in the Right Media Activities with Your Child

During a brief season of my childhood, Sunday nights revolved around the TV. Our family would sit down together and turn on *Lois & Clark*, the show that made Dean Cain and Teri Hatcher famous. I was pretty sure my brother had a crush on Teri Hatcher and that my sister couldn't get enough of Dean Cain, especially with his shirt off. Watching the show became a family tradition. Even my parents would join in and we'd turn it into a family night of sorts. Mom would often pop popcorn in one of those old popcorn popper machines with the little cup on top to melt the butter, and we'd drink grape juice made from the grapes we picked every summer at a vineyard up the hill. I have nothing but good memories of those long-ago Sunday nights, as long as we didn't miss *Lois & Clark*.

I think part of the good memories I have with those Sunday nights was due to the fact that my parents watched with us. Because we did it as a family, we all looked forward to it. It seems to me, looking back now, that experiences like this became more enjoyable simply because Mom and Dad watched with us kids. In fact, when we look back at our childhoods, don't we remember the times our parents either were or were not there? Don't we as parents want to provide good memories for our kids that include doing things together as a family? Things are more fun for kids when parents are involved. But the mere presence of a parent creates more than just fun. It does something else for kids, something pretty amazing, actually.

Partly because of these memories—of doing things with my family—I decided to take my two oldest daughters on a hike during the summer of 2016. This was no ordinary, run-of-the-mill hike, though. We were headed to the top of Texas. To Guadalupe Peak, the highest point elevation-wise in the state of Texas. Those of you in mountain states may be laughing right now. A mountain, in Texas? The joke in the city where we live is that if you stand on a dime, you can see all the way to Dallas—a five-hour drive. That's not true, of course, but it is pretty flat in our part of the country. Guadalupe Peak sits in Guadalupe Mountains National Park, about forty-five minutes southwest of Carlsbad Caverns. We drove to the park on a Tuesday afternoon and set up camp. The next morning, we had the tent put away and the car loaded before the sun came up. We parked at the trailhead and started on the hike at dawn. No more than fifteen minutes up, the trail became very steep, causing one of my daughter's asthma to flare up. We sat down for a few minutes, she took three puffs from her inhaler, and within a short time, we were on the trail again. About an hour into the hike, we encountered a sign warning us of a cliff up ahead. Sure enough, we rounded a corner and found ourselves on a rock ledge about four-feet wide, without a rail to protect us from a cliff that dropped off for hundreds of feet. To make matters worse, the wind was blowing about forty miles per hour. You should know that one of my daughters is scared of heights. She's gets it from me. Heights are not, to put it nicely, my favorite thing. So, we held hands and kept our free hands touching the rock wall next to us as we scooted along the ledge. About thirty steps got us to the other side of the cliff, where we sat down. My daughter—the one that's afraid of heights—put her head in her hands and with a look of sheer terror on her face, told me she wasn't going any further. To be honest, I was pretty scared myself. We sat for a few minutes and then I pointed out a tree line up ahead on the trail. I suggested that we make it to the tree line to see if the trees protected us any better from the wind. They did, so I convinced her to keep going.

The hike didn't get much easier, but having crossed one major obstacle, my daughter's confidence began to grow. We took a break at a ridge we aptly named "pee ridge" since we all took a pee break there, and then kept going. Two hours later, and about 2,500 feet higher, we were approaching the top of the 8,000-foot-plus peak. About 50 yards from the top of the mountain, we came to another set of rock ledges with pretty precipitous drop-offs. My poor daughter began to cry, saying she just wanted to get down off the stupid mountain. "Why is this mountain even here?" she complained. Just then, I looked up and saw the triangle-shaped monument marking the top of the peak about 20 feet over our heads. We scrambled up the last few feet and shouted for joy that we had accomplished our goal. We made it to the top. It took us just over 3 hours to traverse about 4.1 miles and gain 3,000 or so feet in elevation. Not the hardest hike in the world, but it wasn't a hike for the faint-hearted either.

This isn't where the story of the hike ends, however. After all, when you climb up, you're really only halfway there, because you still have to hike back down. We descended, crossing the same two cliff areas. But this time, my daughter held her tongue. She kept her fears at bay. She was more confident in her ability to keep herself safe. On the way down, she told me that she realized that when she doesn't panic, things are easier. She could breathe easier and think easier. She did something that helped her overcome a fear. She did something hard. Really hard. And I was so proud of her. Which leads us, in a somewhat roundabout way, to Media Parenting Strategy #4:

## Media Parenting Strategy #4:
## Participate in the Right Media Activities with Your Child

Here's where we relate this story back to children and media, and to make the connection we'll talk about something researchers call coviewing. Coviewing refers to the simple act of a parent consuming media alongside a child. Coviewing could be watching a TV show or a movie together, playing games or watching YouTube videos together on the tablet, competing against each other in a video game. Coviewing, however, is completely different than parent-child discussions about media that we talked about in Chapter 6. While parent-child discussions about media often occur, coviewing involves just the mere act of participating in a media activity together—without any supplemental conversation, instruction, or discussion. You may wonder how just watching something together can make any difference for the child, but media research suggests that coviewing actually has a pretty significant impact on how children are affected by media exposure.

Coviewing is probably the most common type of media parenting. A majority of parents participate in coviewing on a regular basis. In other words, much of children's television or other media exposure occurs jointly with a coviewing parent. That is for sure the case in my family. In our home, the TV usually doesn't come on until after dinner when all homework and other expectations are done. It's usually during mid-evening, just before kids' bedtimes, that we all just need a break, to sit down and decompress. Often, that happens in front of the TV. I'm not ashamed to admit it. These viewing experiences tend to be family-viewing experiences. Our kids don't have TVs or computers in their bedrooms, so if they want to watch TV or play on the tablet or get on the Internet, we are usually either close by or we are doing it together. As we've already discussed, children's viewing habits tend to somewhat mirror their parents' media habits, and this often results in doing media-related activities together.

Just as watching *Lois & Clark* with my parents seemed to make the activity more enjoyable for me, research shows that the mere presence of a coviewing parent can enhance the effects of media exposure. For example, *Sesame Street* is perhaps the most well-known and most-researched children's educational program. One study found that children learned more from watching the show when their parent was simply in the room, even when their parent didn't utter a single word to the child about the content.[1] Other research found that children's vocabulary learned while watching *Sesame Street* improved when they watched the show with their parent.[2] This is good news for parents and provides very practical implications. If you want your child to learn more from media exposure, simply participate in the media activity with them. How hard is that, really? You don't have to say a word. You simply need to be present. The world's children could benefit from more parents who are simply present.

On the other hand, you may have already figured out that if the presence of the parent can enhance children's learning from educational television, it can also enhance children's learning of other content—for good or ill. For example, children who watched a short, five-minute clip of a violent cartoon with a coviewing parent exhibited greater aggressive tendencies than children who watched without a parent.[3] And children who regularly watch TV in the presence of a coviewing parent were found to be nearly four times as likely to experience fear in response to television content than children whose parents do not regularly coview TV with them.[4] These findings are also true for adolescents. When their parent coviews television with them, teenagers are more likely to endorse stereotypical gender roles and to be more afraid of the outside world.[5]

Why, though, does the presence of a parent change how children are affected by media exposure? Yes, it makes the experience more enjoyable, and when content is more enjoyable children might pay more attention to it, and thus, learn more. But is that the only explanation? Remember the hike up to Guadalupe Peak with my daughters? Because we did the hike together, my daughter's experience with cliffs was different on the way down than it was on the way up. She had learned to see the cliffs differently. Because of her experience going up, with me at her side holding her hand, she could navigate the trip on the way down by herself. Her perception of the cliff, and of herself, changed. In other words, the way her brain processed the information in front of her changed. And that resulted in her feeling calmer. She didn't have the same feelings of panic. She could see the situation more clearly, without the fog that comes with panic and fear. Said differently, her body's physiological reaction to the cliff areas on our hike changed because of how my presence on the way up changed how she perceived the hike.

Let's relate this to coviewing, then. Why does the mere presence of a coviewing parent alter children's learning from media exposure? There are two theories that have been posited by researchers to help explain the effects of coviewing, though as far as I know, only one of these theories has actually been tested. The first, untested theory, suggests that the presence of a parent during media exposure signals to the child that the parent approves of the content, approves of the child watching the content, and that the content is worthy of the child's attention.[6] If the child makes these assumptions, whether consciously or not, the theory suggests that the child will pay more attention to the content, and thus be more affected by it. To me, this is a plausible, logical explanation. But I like the second theory better, and not just because it relates to my daughter's experience climbing Guadalupe Peak.

Research on a psychological phenomenon called "social facilitation" dates back to the 1800s. Scientists discovered that people could reel in a fishing line faster if they did it with someone in the room with them. Similarly, scientists noticed that people could race faster on a bicycle when they did it against someone in competition. I'm not a great runner, but I have run a few distance races, and I've noticed that when I'm about to pass a group of spectators, especially people I know, I tend to pick up my pace a bit. I remember running in a high school track meet. I wasn't the fastest kid, so I was thrown in with the long-distance runners. Every time around the track, we'd pass in front of the grandstands. I always straightened up just a little bit, ran a little faster, and pretended to not be in such pain. I also recently ran a marathon. In the last mile, I could only walk because of cramping in my legs. But as I neared the finish line where my family and other spectators were, I was able to make my body run the last few hundred yards without any cramping. Similarly, social facilitation theory suggests that people tend to perform better on simple tasks when they do the tasks in the presence of another person. The reason for this improved performance is because the presence of another person increases the physiological arousal levels of an individual. Heightened physiological arousal is a fancy way of saying that our bodies are "ready to go." Our bodies respond according to the circumstances we encounter. When our bodies are at a heightened level of arousal, we tend to focus better, learn better, devote our efforts to the task more efficiently, and ultimately, perform better at the task (especially if the task is easy, like watching TV).

A strong connection exists between our mind's perception of things and our physiological arousal. For example, our heart rate increases when we watch a scary movie, even though we know it's not true. When we're anticipating an important event, we might become fidgety and our palms might start to sweat. Before every high school basketball game, I remember having to go to the bathroom five or six times before running out onto the court. Maybe you took piano lessons and your hands started to shake and sweat before the piano recital. That is simply the manifestation of the connection between our minds and our bodies. Social scientists suggest that this connection is innate in humans and serves as a protection for us. This is the same process that drives our fight-or-flight tendencies. When we perceive that something might be harmful, our body kicks itself into avoidance mode. We become more aware of our surroundings, and as one of my colleagues put it, our body prepares itself to fight against a tiger that is trying to rip our face off. On the other hand, when pleasant things happen in our environment, such as a hug from a child, watching friends play horseshoes, or smelling the magnolia on the breeze, our body has a similar reaction. But, instead of a heightened awareness that avoids the stimulus, we have a heightened awareness that results in what are called "approach tendencies." Our bodies prepare themselves to learn more, explore, engage more with the pleasant stimulus. And these responses are manifest in measurable ways, such as through our heart rate.

If this is the case, it makes sense that the mere presence of a coviewing parent may be perceived as a pleasant environmental stimulus for a child, thereby affecting children's physiological arousal and activating this approach tendency. This approach tendency would cause the child to engage more with the media content, to expend more cognitive effort trying to understand it, and thereby learn more from it. Wondering if this was actually the case, my colleagues and I designed a study to test the theory.[7] We invited more than eighty parent-child pairs into a research lab at Texas Tech. The lab was set up like a typical living room, with a couch and loveseat, a big screen TV, a couple of lamps, and a coffee table. We had some kids watch a twelve-minute clip of a TV show by themselves, and we had other kids watch the clip with their parent sitting next to them on the couch. We instructed each parent who sat next to the child to not say anything to the child during the show. For all the kids, we attached heart-rate and skin-conductance (palm sweat) sensors and monitored them as they watched the show. The results were astounding. Children who watched the show in the presence of their silent, coviewing parent, exhibited lower heart rates and higher skin conductance. In other words, the mere presence of a coviewing parent resulted in lower heart rates for children, which indicates heightened physiological arousal, and more palm sweat, which indicates greater cognitive resource allocation, or how much mental effort they devoted to the task (watching TV).

How cool is that? Simply watching TV with children can alter their physiology. Years of research shows that these changes in physiology are highly related to how hard the mind works to process and understand something, including media content. It's no wonder, then, that children learn better from media when a parent watches with them. Their body is more ready to learn more. As far as I know, this is the only study that has measured the effect of a coviewing parent on children's physiological arousal. And although it is only one study with only one medium (television), it is a great improvement in our understanding of how the simple act of coviewing is related to children being more affected by media exposure. Remember the caveat, however. The same processes that have been shown to be at play with positive media content are also in play with negative media content. In other words, the presence of a parent can enhance children's learning of both "good" content and "bad" content. That's why Media Parenting Strategy #4 includes the word *right*: "participate in the *right* media activities with your child."

Most of the research related to coviewing relates to television. Much less research involves coplaying video games or other newer technology. In addition, much less research looks at outcomes beyond the classic outcomes associated with viewing violent, sexual, or persuasive media content. In recent years, researchers have begun to explore how coviewing, or coplaying, impacts the parent-child relationship. Is it possible that simply spending time together doing something that both parent and child enjoy can help them feel closer to each other? Based on my experiences with our Sunday *Lois & Clark* nights, it sure makes a lot of sense. And research suggests that such outcomes can occur.

I'll refer to another study led by Dr. Sarah Coyne to illustrate how parent-child relationships can be changed by coplaying. Dr. Coyne and her colleagues had 287 adolescents ages 11–16 and their parents complete questionnaires designed to tap into certain family processes and adolescent behaviors.[8] The study found that the more often girls coplayed video games with their parents, especially age-appropriate games, the higher their level of parent-child connectedness was. The authors argued that when parents coplay video games with their daughters, they are sending one of several messages. First, the authors suggested, playing together sends the message to the daughter that the parent values the activities that are important to her. Next, coplaying allows opportunities for parent-daughter conversations to take place that may not otherwise happen. Maybe there is something about the activity of playing video games that breaks down certain conversational barriers. The study also found, interestingly, that girls who coplayed video games with a parent had lower levels of internalizing symptoms, such as depression and anxiety, as well as lower levels of aggressive behavior. They also displayed more prosocial behaviors, such as kindness and generosity, toward family members. Coplaying, at least for girls, seems to be a way in which parents can create emotional bonds with their daughters.

We've now talked about coviewing TV and coplaying video games. Let's talk now about one of the most common parent-child media activities: reading books together. Like many parents, there are some books in my house that I've read so many times that I think I might spontaneously combust if I have to read them again: *Green Eggs and Ham. Good Night Moon.* And that book about loving you to the moon and back. Research shows that kids need the parent-child interaction that happens while reading books together, above and beyond the actual words in the books. Reading books with kids is different than watching TV with them. TV encourages us to sit there, be quiet, and watch. In fact, I sort of hate it when my kids talk to me when I'm trying to pay attention to something we're watching on TV. When I read books with my youngest daughter, however, I am constantly asking and responding to questions (at least that's what happens when I'm in a good mood and have enough energy! I've actually fallen asleep in the middle of reading a book to my child, as I'm sure many other tired parents have). A 2011 study with which I was involved explored these differences in detail.[9] Led by Dr. Amy Nathanson at The Ohio State University, seventy-three children (preschoolers and toddlers) and each of their mothers came to a lab on campus and either (1) read books together, (2) watched TV together, or (3) played with toys together. Participants were videotaped during the thirty-minute session, and researchers counted every act of communication between the mother and the child. Each mother-child interaction during the session was categorized for how "responsive" the mother's communication was. Examples of responsive communication included asking questions, providing affirmations of the child's communication, imitating the child's communication, and responding to the child, instead of simply providing information to the child. Children were also interviewed to assess their early literacy skills. Results showed that mothers communicated significantly more with their child when they read books with them compared to when they watched TV with them, and that takes into account the communication used to actually read the stories. The same was true for playing with toys with kids. In addition, mothers' communication was much more responsive, or sophisticated, while reading books than while playing with toys or watching TV. Why is this important? Because, the study showed, the sophistication of mothers' communication to children was related to some aspects of children's emerging literacy skills. Early literacy skills, in turn, are related to academic and reading achievement. In other words, shared book reading—a form of coviewing or joint media engagement—allows for opportunities to share more sophisticated communication than talk that happens during coviewing of television.

So, let's talk about some media parenting takeaways from what we know about coviewing now. If parents are going to help their kids navigate the media maze, coviewing must be strategic. Based on the research we've reviewed here, and some we haven't, I recommend the following as it relates to coviewing:

**Bring the TV out of the bedroom and into a shared space.** When I was young, I remember our family having just one television, and it was in a shared space like the family room. Today, televisions are cheaper. What's more, television content doesn't need to come through a box on the wall—it can come through a smart phone, tablet, or other personal device. This means that opportunities for coviewing, or joint media engagement, are fewer and farther between. If parents want to help kids learn simply by participating jointly in a media activity, the media activity must occur in a shared space.

**Find media activities that your child enjoys and spend time participating with them.** A couple of my daughters enjoy watching a YouTube channel called "Brooklyn and Bailey." It includes videos by twin sisters, Brooklyn and Bailey (of course), who talk about things important to tween girls, like how to do different hairstyles, fun competitions like the polar bear plunge or a gross jelly bean challenge, fashion, crafts, costumes, and do-it-yourself holiday decorations. This would be very hard for me to get into. For better or for worse, when it comes to media, I am the stereotypical male—I like sports, tools, and monkeys picking at each other's butts. New hairstyles, not so much. Scrapbooking, never. Nail polish, I leave the room as fast as I can, even if it's on TV. I swear I can smell it through the screen. Watching this YouTube channel with them would take superhuman effort for me. It will probably never happen. But, maybe there are some other media activities that I can do with my daughters. Something they enjoy that I also enjoy. Like watching funny animal videos. We enjoy a skateboarding dog, and dog-shaming videos. My daughters also seem to gravitate toward the laptop when I watch videos of athletic events, such as the Olympic trials, especially when the events involve women. I can get into those things with them. I don't need to share every minute of their media time, but I can share some of the time.

**Create media-related family traditions.** On one or two Friday nights per month, put in a Redbox movie, or as more tech-savvy people do it, watch a movie together on Netflix. Be sure the movies are kid appropriate, of course. Whether or not your kids learn something from the movie, I believe family movie time is worth it in order to create a stronger feeling of unity in the family, simply because everyone is doing something that everyone enjoys, together. I've also created a cool media tradition with my youngest daughter. One day we were flipping through channels and we came across PBS's *Nature*, a show about all things, well, nature. Together we've learned about mule deer, dolphins, butterflies, hummingbirds, gorillas, giant armadillos, and a host of other creatures. We've learned to identify when animals are "making babies" (if it's too graphic, we change the channel for a few minutes), and we've learned how humans can coexist with animals. Watching *Nature* has become a tradition for us, and I hope she'll look back fondly at these weekly joint-learning experiences.

**Remember that coviewing alone is not enough.** In your efforts to be a more active participant in your child's media activities, remember that coviewing is not enough. We've already talked quite a bit about the power of parent-child conversations about media. When you watch, play, or read together, it is well worth the effort to provide additional information, share opinions, and ask questions. These conversations have been shown to negate the negative effect that coviewing can have when children are exposed to potentially negative media content, and they have been shown to help facilitate children's adoption of potentially positive media messages.

**Invite your kids to be involved with your media experiences.** This piece of advice is only valid if you follow Media Parenting Strategy #1— alter your own media habits. One of my favorite things to do online is watch people under anesthesia. For real. Google it. There are some great videos of people waking up after getting their wisdom teeth removed. My wife and I have shared more than one date night sitting on our bed watching anesthesia videos together. Whenever I'm online and something makes me laugh, in no less than five seconds I usually have at least two of my four kids looking over my shoulder. I wish they jumped to attention that fast when I ask them to help clear the table. In fact, one day not too long ago while I was eating lunch, I was watching something on my laptop that simply made noise. Heaven forbid. My daughter heard the noise and left her lunch to look at what I was watching online. Kids want to spend time with their parents. They want to laugh with us. They want to know what we know. They ask all those questions for a reason. Yes, one thousand questions every day is tough to handle, and I'm convinced we as parents need time away from our kids in order to maintain some semblance of sanity. I am probably the most ardent supporter of having adult time away from the kids. But, when I'm at home doing something with media, what does it hurt to have my kids involved? Sure, that might mean that they might take up our space on the couch and breathe in our ear. But I hear through the grapevine that it is precisely those things—their smell, their presence, their noise, and their laughter—that we'll miss the most when they're grown and gone. I share this advice not only with you, but with myself. I am selfish, too selfish, with my time and my space. Inviting my kids to join me in with what I'm doing online, on my phone, or on TV can have so many benefits. It's time to start self-sacrificing a little bit for their benefit, and for ours.

**When you do use the TV as a babysitter, at least be in the same room.** My wife and I, with four kids, know just as well as other parents that sometimes we have to use the TV as a babysitter. Sometimes, it is just easier to put in a movie so that we can get something done. In fact, while I'm sitting at my computer typing this paragraph, my two youngest daughters are watching *Big Hero 6*. I did that on purpose, because without the TV on, they'd be talking to me, and I'd never get this book written. Kind of ironic that in order to write a book about better media parenting, I've plopped my kids in front of the TV. Sometimes, though, it's just necessary. I'm okay with that. I tell the guilt that pops up when I do use the TV as a babysitter to go away. But when we do use the TV as a babysitter, we can at least be in the same room. I'm sitting at the kitchen bar right now. The carpet to the family room starts about three feet behind me and there is no wall between me, my kids, or the TV. We're in the same room. Every now and then they interrupt me with a "did you see that?" or "Dad, the DVD is scratched, can you come fix it?" And that's okay. I get something done and I'm still kind of here. I still know what they're watching. I can still answer questions. I'd like to think that they still get the benefits of coviewing because I am here with them. If not, at least I'm still here with them, and that counts for something, right?

Despite what I know about coviewing, I recently made a media-parenting mistake. You'll see that I made up for it, but it still bothers me. One morning, I was sitting in my kitchen working on my computer when my daughter came and told me something I never thought I would hear. "Dad, did you know that there's such a thing as a narwhal with two horns?" she asked. No, I did not know that. In fact, turns out there are a lot of things about narwhals that I don't know, but I soon found out, because before I knew it, she had me looking up photos of narwhals online, including a search for an apparently rare, two-horned narwhal. Did you know that narwhals are so rare that they are sometimes called the "unicorns of the sea"? It took the curiosity of a first grader to teach me this. Kids seem to be naturally curious, and what we do with that curiosity seems to make a big difference.[10]

Now, here's my moment of regret. After just a couple of minutes of looking up information about narwhals that day, I went right back to my work. Apparently, my "deadline" was more important than time spent helping my daughter learn more about something cool. But based on what we know about media parenting by now—that parents can help kids learn more from the media than they ever could alone—I decided to make it up to her later by sharing with her a fact I learned online that afternoon about narwhals. Did you know that narwhal tusks can breathe in seawater, giving the narwhal information about the water's temperature and saltiness? Neither did I. But I do now, and so does my daughter. We used media together to learn something pretty darn cool.

## Conclusion

We've now talked about four different media parenting strategies—strategies that will help you help your children navigate the media maze. The ultimate goal of these media parenting strategies, and of parenting in general, is to prepare kids to become productive and educated adults themselves. These strategies are designed to do one thing: help kids become more critical consumers of media. By critical consumers, I mean that talking to kids about media, setting media rules the right way, using media with them, and changing our own media habits is all aimed at helping kids be able to make media-related choices that will enhance their well-being and help them navigate the media maze in a healthy way. In order to make those choices, they need to be able to discern when they might be persuaded, why certain messages may be inappropriate, and what subtle things media producers do to deceive. They need to realize when they are being affected by media exposure. In other words, all these efforts are to help our kids become media literate. And there is nobody in a better position to help make this happen than media-literate parents.

Notes
1.  John Wright, Michelle St. Peters, and Aletha Huston, "Family Television Use and Its Relation to Children's Cognitive Skills and Social Behavior," in *Television and the American Family*, ed. Jennings Bryant (Hillsdale, NJ: Lawrence Erlbaum Associates, 1990), 227-251.
2.  Mabel Rice et al., "Words From 'Sesame Street': Learning Vocabulary While Viewing," *Developmental Psychology* 26, no. 3 (1990): 421-428, doi: 10.1037/0012-1649.26.3.421.

3. Amy Nathanson, "Identifying and Explaining the Relationship Between Parental Mediation and Children's Aggression," *Communication Research* 26, no. 2 (1999): 124-143, doi: 10.1177/009365099026002002.

4. E Paavonen et al., "Do Parental Co-Viewing and Discussions Mitigate TV-Induced Fears in Young Children?" *Child: Care Health and Development* 35, no. 6 (2009): 773-780, doi: 10.1111/j.1365-2214.2009.01009.x.

5. Nancy Rothschild and Michael Morgan, "Cohesion and Control: Adolescents' Relationships with Parents as Mediators of Television," *Journal of Early Adolescence* 7, no. 3 (1987): 299-314, doi: 10.1177/0272431687073006.

6. Amy Nathanson, "Mediation of Children's Television Viewing: Working toward Conceptual Clarity and Common Understanding," in *Communication Yearbook 25*, ed. William Gudykunst (Mahwah, NJ: Lawrence Erlbaum Associates, 2001), 115-151, doi: 10.1080/23808985.2001.11679002.

7. Eric Rasmussen et al., "Explaining Parental Coviewing: The Role of Social Facilitation and Arousal," *Communication Monographs* (2016): 1-20, doi: 10.1080/03637751.2016.1259532.

8. Sarah Coyne et al., "Game On . . . Girls: Associations Between Co-Playing Video Games and Adolescent Behavioral and Family Outcomes," *Journal of Adolescent Health* 49, no. 2 (2011): 160-165, doi: 10.1016/j.jadohealth.2010.11.249.

9. Amy Nathanson and Eric Rasmussen, "TV Viewing Compared to Book Reading and Toy Playing Reduces Responsive Maternal Communication With Toddlers and Preschoolers," *Human Communication Research* 37, no. 4 (2011): 465-487, doi: 10.1111/j.1468-2958.2011.01413.x.

10. To learn more about how kids learn about science, see Joyce Alexander, Kathy Johnson, and Ken Kelley, "Longitudinal Analysis of the Relations Between Opportunities to Learn About Science and the Development of Interests Related to Science," *Science Education* 96, no. 5 (2012): 763-786, doi: 10.1002/sce.21018. In this study of 215 4-year-olds, researchers found that kids who expressed interest in science-related subjects at age four were more likely to use media to seek out science-related information at ages 6 and 7. These science-related media activities (reading and watching TV), in turn, stimulated more science-related questions. In other words, when kids express an interest in science, they tend to turn to media to help answer their questions. And what they find in the media tends to inspire even more science-related questions.

# 9 Conclusion
## Current and Future Issues with Children and Media Research

Okay, let's say we do everything we talked about in previous chapters. We change our own media habits. We have effective conversations with our kids about what they see in the media. We set the right rules in the right way. And we engage strategically in joint parent-child media activities with our kids. Our hope is that we prevent our kids from experiencing negative media effects. We also hope that we can help our kids enjoy all the good that can be found in the media. In other words, we do this all in an effort to positively influence our kids' well-being. That's the ultimate goal, right?

Almost.

I say "almost" because at the deepest of levels, what we're really trying to do is influence who our kids *become*, isn't it? And when we talk of who our kids are and who we hope they'll become, we're talking about much more than changing their attitudes and behaviors. We're talking bigger things, like character, identity, and heart. And those things—character, identity, and heart—are pretty hard to quantify. Admittedly, it's tough to measure the goodness or resilience of one's character. I wouldn't know how to start measuring someone's faith, their innermost desires, or the amount of unconditional love in their heart. So, how can we know if our media parenting efforts make a difference where it really counts? How can we know if we're having any influence on who our kids are becoming?

Because these important, soul-deep things are so nebulous and difficult to pin down, our conversations in this chapter will need to leave the safe confines of science and personal anecdotes to which we've become accustomed in this book. To understand *becoming*, we need to spend a little time off the paved scientific road, and in the scientific bushes, by talking about some topics that science has a hard time explaining. We'll first discuss a few things that we know about the human brain—that all-important but little understood command center for our bodies. And then we'll really get into the fringes—and the future—of science by addressing what until now has been perceived as a taboo topic in the scientific circles in which I run: the human "mind" or "soul." Finally, we'll wrap things with a conversation about who our kids really are.

## The Biases in Our Brains

Sprained ankles are no fun. But they can teach us something about the brain.

In the 2017 NBA playoffs, the Golden State Warriors played the San Antonio Spurs in the Western Conference finals. If this language is foreign to some, we're talking about basketball. Two really good basketball teams played each other. During the course of the game, the best player on the Spurs, Kawhi Leonard, went up for a jump shot near the left sideline. The defender, Zaza Pachulia, ran toward Leonard. His momentum carried him somewhat under Leonard, and when Leonard came down, his foot landed on top of Pachulia's foot. If you've ever played a sport and landed on someone else's foot, you know what happens. Leonard sprained his ankle, of course. Pachulia had done something called "entering the landing space of the shooter." After the game, the coach of the Spurs, Gregg Popovich, went on an epic rant about how Pachulia tried to purposely injure Leonard. Meanwhile, Pachulia denied any wrongdoing and basically said that he didn't even know Leonard had landed on his foot until he saw Leonard writhing in pain on the ground.

Who was right? Did Pachulia intend to hurt Leonard, or was it an honest mistake? I've watched the video of what happened several times, and I don't know the answer. I suppose only Pachulia will ever know. But everyone else *thinks* they know. Depending on who you ask, the answer will be different. With their last dying breath, Spurs fans will blame Pachulia for purposefully hurting his opponent, while Warriors fans will defend Pachulia with the same amount of conviction. Fans' brains are simply biased. They see their team through a lens that isn't quite clear. Is there any way to see the situation objectively? I suppose that's what referees are for. But then again, referees are still human and are subject to biases just like anybody else.

Our brains are clouded by our opinions. The biases that reside in our brains prevent us from seeing the world clearly. We could argue, then, that unless we can really, truly see with total objectivity, we are not really free from bias. In other words, our biases limit our *freedom* to see things for what they really are. They limit our brains. They limit the ability of our brains to function freely. We could even say that the only brain that is free is the brain that contains no bias.

Here's another classic example that demonstrates the same principle about the biases that reside in our brains. In the fall of 1951, Dartmouth and Princeton played a football game against each other.[1] Princeton's All-American quarterback, Richard Kazmaier, had just appeared on the cover of *TIME* Magazine and had led his team to an undefeated record heading into the game. The game turned into what might rightly be called a bloodbath. Kazmaier's nose was broken, and a Dartmouth player had his leg broken. So violent was the game that the Princeton student newspaper described the game as "a disgusting exhibition of so-called 'sport,'"[2] and blamed the Dartmouth players for letting their lack of sportsmanship get out of control. And, to nobody's surprise, Dartmouth fans were equally vehement in their accusations of the dirty way in which Princeton played the game. Because of the distinctness of the level of violence in this game, researchers decided to conduct a study. One week after the game, researchers showed a video of the game to students at each school and asked them to identify any rules infractions, and to label the infractions as either mild or flagrant. Again, not surprisingly, Princeton students said the Dartmouth football players committed more than twice as many penalties as players on their own team. And Dartmouth students said they thought both sides were to blame, and that Princeton fans were just mad that their star player got hurt. The authors concluded that "results indicate that the 'game' was actually many different games and that each version of the events that transpired was just as 'real' to a particular person as other versions were to other people."[3]

Once again, we ask the question, who was right? Princeton fans or Dartmouth fans? Both? Neither? Here's the all-important question then: are our brains completely free from bias? And the answer is, probably not. In some way, we are each held captive by our brains. And that's where media parenting can make a big difference.

## Rewiring the Brain

The human brain is an amazing thing. I'm not a brain researcher, but from what I've read, we know that the brain is the body's command center and that it keeps our vital organs working. We also know that our brains can be trained. For example, researchers reviewed dozens of studies related to the brain's response to cognitive and motor skills training and found that our brains actually change when we learn information.[4] When we become good at a task—like driving a car or typing on a keyboard—our brains don't need to work as hard at completing the task. After training and becoming good at something, the regions of the brain that help manage attention-demanding tasks are less active, while regions of the brain that are normally resting are more active.[5] In other words, our brains change the way they work based on the information we put into them.

I'm not an addiction expert either, but research I've read suggests that the structure and function of our brains change when we become addicted to something, such as drugs, alcohol, gambling, shopping, or sex.[6] Using addiction as an example is an extreme case, of course, but people lose much of their freedom to choose whether or not they will participate in an activity once they are addicted because of how addiction changes the brain.

What we put into our minds changes our brains. And changes to our brain can change who we, and our children, *become*. The brain is so susceptible to the messages that it encounters that an entirely new field called "neuromarketing" has risen in popularity in recent years. Neuromarketing is "the application of neuroimaging techniques to sell products."[7] As they have for decades, advertisers want to develop the most persuasive marketing message or advertisement possible. They want their advertisements to get as close as possible to hitting our brain's "buy button." Neuromarketers know that certain parts of our brains are related to emotion and impulse. They know that certain regions are associated with both predictable and unpredictable choices, and other regions with pleasure and reward.[8] And they know that different messages influence different parts of our brain. So, they tailor their messages to the parts of our brain that they want to activate and that may make us more likely to buy their products. In essence, they want to hijack our brains, and research shows that they're pretty good at it.

For example, in one study, participants (all healthy adults) were shown pictures and prices of products while in an fMRI machine that measured activity in various parts of their brains.[9] Participants then indicated whether or not they would buy the product. Results showed that certain parts of the brain were activated, and certain parts were not, when people decided to make a purchasing decision. Specifically, if we're going to get technical, the region of the brain called the nucleus accumbens was more active during the phase of the study in which participants were making their purchase decision. At the same time, the region of the brain called the insula was less active when participants decided *not* to buy the product. This is highly valuable information for neuromarketers—if they want to convince someone to buy their product, they simply need to design a message that helps keep the insula active at the point of purchase.

In another study, fifteen healthy women were placed in an fMRI machine and were shown a series of six advertisements related to a chocolate product.[10] Each ad was just a bit different than the others. After seeing the six ads, participants ranked which image they liked best. Meanwhile, researchers also placed six different corresponding advertising displays in a supermarket—a different one each week for six weeks—and measured sales of the product. Results showed that researchers were able to very accurately predict which areas of the brain would be most activated with each type of ad, and thus were able to forecast sales.

Boiled down, neuromarketing research shows that our brains respond in predictable ways to different stimuli. If producers of media content can create a message that targets certain parts of the brain, the message has the ability to grab our attention and to help persuade us to change our behaviors. In some way, then, media messages have the ability to take away some of our freedom to make objective choices because they change our brain. And once our brains change due to something we've seen in the media, they can no longer see the world in the same way.

Because of our brain's ability to change, experts say our brains are "plastic." Not plastic in the sense that they're made of plastic, of course, but plastic in the sense that they are moldable, that they change every time we learn something. Researchers suggest that our brains are made of a system of connecting neurons, like a system of roads throughout a city—they're all connected. To illustrate these neuron connections, let's do a short experiment.[11] I didn't make this experiment up, but play along with me here. It will help illustrate the point I'm trying to make. I'm going to share a word or short phrase. When you see the word/short phrase, I want you to raise your *right* hand as fast as you can if you think that the thing is good. And if you think the word is bad, raise your *left* hand as fast as you can. Good = right hand up fast. Bad = left hand up fast. Easy enough, right?

Ready?

Here we go. The word is *cockroach*.

What did you do? I'm guessing your left hand went up pretty fast.

Okay, here's another word/phrase. Remember, good = right hand up fast. Bad = left hand up fast. Ready? Here it is: *your second grade teacher*.

What happened? I'm guessing your right hand went up, but that it went up more slowly than your left hand did when you read "cockroach." This is an example of the connections our brains make between neurons. Somewhere in our brain is stored our opinion about cockroaches. When your eyes saw the word *cockroach*, your brain hurriedly scoured its neurons and found your negative opinion about cockroaches pretty quickly. But when you read the words *your second grade teacher*, your brain had to work a little bit harder, a little bit longer, to find your opinion about your second grade teacher. It wasn't a straight shot to find your opinion about your second grade teacher. In other words, the link between your mental representation of cockroach and your attitude about cockroaches is pretty strong. On the other hand, the link between the mental representation of your second grade teacher and your opinion of your second grade teacher is much weaker since it's been so long since you've had to think about both. It's weaker because our brains are plastic. Our brains change and rewire themselves. Links between neurons can be strengthened or weakened due to the passage of time, or due to the messages we put into our brains.

Let's illustrate this with another example. As I've mentioned before, where I live, it's extremely flat. I cannot see a single mountain, hill, or knoll from my house. So when it rains, there is no place for the water to go and we end up with a bunch of flooded intersections and streets. One time our daughter was at a birthday party at a home less than a mile from our house. Just before we were supposed to pick her up, it started raining. Hard. Like, torrentially. Normally, it would take three minutes at the most to pick her up—it's a pretty straight shot between our house and the house where the birthday party was. But on this night, the road we would normally take was flooded with several feet of water. It was completely impassable. Several people tried to drive their cars through the water, but their cars either stalled or were swept into the ditch. I had to borrow my neighbor's jacked-up pickup to make a four-mile detour through flooded streets and intersections just to go one half mile "as the crow flies." A trip that should have taken three minutes took fifteen minutes. I had to reroute the driving directions because something was in the way. Our brains work similarly. When we are repeatedly exposed to something, or when that something (such as a cockroach) elicits a particularly powerful reaction in us, the link between our mental representation of that thing and our attitude about that thing can be pretty strong. It doesn't take long for our brains to make the connection between the two. It's like the roads aren't flooded. But, with the passage of time, when it's been thirty years (gasp!) since we've seen our second grade teacher, that connection is weakened. It's like a rainstorm has come in and flooded the streets in our brain, and our brain has to find a workaround to get to our attitude about that thing.

But not all brain rewiring is bad. Mindfulness training shows that what we put into our brain can change the structure and function of our brains in a positive way. Mindfulness training seems to be increasingly popular as a way to help people cope with stress. I'm not an expert on mindfulness, but it is described as a way of thinking about, concentrating on, and paying attention to one's "inner and outer experiences in a non-judgmental manner from moment to moment."[12] Mindfulness interventions can include meditation, body scanning, and mindful yoga as ways of letting go of tension and other emotions in the body.[13] Research shows that mindfulness therapies can actually change our brains. For example, one study found that after eight weeks of mindfulness training, regions of the brain known to be associated with one's attention-regulation ability, perspective taking, and self-awareness experienced greater stimulation.[14] In addition, mindfulness training affects the efficiency of the region of the brain called the amygdala, the region of the brain that regulates emotion.[15] Based on the study's results, it appears that mindfulness training helps redirect our brains' responses to stressful stimuli away from the amygdala to other parts of the brain, thereby allowing us to take a more thoughtful, less emotional approach to stressful stimuli. In other words, mindfulness therapies help our brains think about things in a way that is less encumbered by emotions.

## Media and Brain Desensitization

Let's connect this discussion back to what we know about media. Let's look at these same concepts through the lens of research into the desensitizing effect of violent media. "Desensitization" means that with repeated exposure to something (such as sex or violence), our minds and bodies do not react the same way they did when we saw the content for the first time.[16] Violence starts to not bother us as much. We don't get as surprised when we see portrayals of sex. Content that was previously objectionable to us is now more acceptable. Said differently, we lose the ability to see the world for what it really is. Our brains are no longer free from outside influence.

Dr. Doug Gentile, a media researcher at Iowa State University, led a study looking at how the brain exhibits desensitization effects.[17] In the study, late adolescents (ages eighteen to twenty-one) who were each classified as "gamers" played both a violent and nonviolent version of the game *Unreal Tournament, 2004*, while undergoing an fMRI scan. Prior to playing, participants reported how often they played violent and nonviolent video games. Half of the participants reported that they mostly played violent games, while the other half had more exposure to nonviolent games. The object of the video game in the experiment was to try to find and capture the other team's flag, kind of like the real-life game of Capture the Flag. In the violent version of the game, participants were instructed to shoot and kill any other person they encountered in the game, including members of their own team. In the nonviolent version of the game, players also held a gun, but it fired discs that did not cause any harm, sort of like paint balls. Comparisons of the brain responses of those who were classified as "violent gamers" before the study versus those who were classified as "nonviolent gamers" found that when playing the violent version of the game, regions of the brain associated with emotional responses were more active among nonviolent gamers and were suppressed with violent gamers. The authors of the study suggest that these results are indicative of "a long-term desensitization effect from prior violent game play."[18] By playing violent video games on a regular basis, gamers are less physiologically aroused by violent games, meaning they don't see violence the same way. They don't experience the same levels of disgust or aversion. Playing violent games has essentially robbed their brains of the ability to see violence for what it is.

## Media Parenting and Children's Brains

So, what does all this brainy mumbo jumbo mean for media parenting? This means that media parenting may be more powerful—much more powerful—than we previously thought. This means that media parenting has the power to prevent media messages from changing children's brains by (1) preventing the message from entering our kids' brains in the first place, or (2) by helping alter the meaning of media messages that do make it into children's brains. By preventing exposure to or changing the meaning of media messages, media parenting, at its deepest level, can actually protect our children's freedom of thought. It can help keep their brains unencumbered by messages that could ultimately affect how they see the world, how they treat other people, and *who they become*. Media parenting can prevent our kids from *becoming* desensitized to negative media content. Media parenting is powerful. And that means that a parent who conscientiously engages in media parenting is a powerful parent. And only powerful parents—parents who rely on themselves, and not on rules or technology to do the job of media parenting—can empower their children to navigate the increasingly complex media maze.

Which brings us right back to where we started at the beginning of this book. One way to protect kids' freedom of mind, and ultimately their character, is to try to completely avoid any and all media. But, as we've discussed, there is no way to do that. So, the only logical way—the way that should no longer seem unconventional at this point—is to empower kids to deal with the messages that have the potential to change their brains. The way to protect our kids' brains, and their freedom of thought, is to empower them with the tools to be able to take in those messages, put them in the proper perspective, and make their own decisions about how to use the information. We do that by setting an example for how the media should, and should not, be integrated into our lives. We do that by talking with them about media. We do that by sharing our opinions about media content with them. We do that by setting rules about media use—and explaining those rules—in a way that supports children's desire to think freely for themselves. We do that by using media together with them, because we know that our presence, just like media messages, can change their brain's reaction to media content. All the research points to the plausibility that our media parenting efforts can break down walls that negative media content puts up in kids' brain mazes. Media parenting, like media messages, can change the way children think. Media parenting can open up new routes in children's brain mazes and help them avoid media dead ends. It can provide easier pathways for kids to be able to see their way through to the end of the maze. In other words, media parenting has the potential to free children's brains from the changes caused by media messages. Media parenting is about enhancing children's freedom of thought. It's about protecting their ability to develop positive character traits. It's about giving our kids the chance to become what we hope they'll become.

Our children have a right to see the world through clear glasses. Not through glasses clouded by the values, morals, and opinions that limit their freedom to think clearly and to *become*. They deserve to be able to see through the opaque walls of the media maze that make it so difficult to navigate life as a child today. And that's really the purpose of media parenting. Media parenting isn't really intended to simply prevent our kids from adopting aggressive attitudes. Media parenting isn't really about keeping our kids from learning unhealthy sexual behaviors. Media parenting *is* about protecting children's minds from influences that restrict their freedom to see the world clearly. And this kind of protection doesn't come by the old way of doing things (simply taking media away or by relying on the old-fashioned way of setting "my-way-or-the-highway" rules). It comes by empowering kids with the tools to navigate the media maze for themselves.

## Media Parenting and Children's "Souls"

When we talk of children's brains, we must also talk of their "mind" or their "soul." If you don't think I'm crazy yet, what I'm about to share might make you wonder about my level of sanity. You might think that I'm saving the crazy for last because I'm hoping people will have stopped reading by now, but the opposite is actually true. I want to share something that will really get parents thinking about kids, about who their kids are, and about who they can become. So, I invite you to hear me out, even if you come away thinking I'm a lunatic. It has much to do with our discussion of the brain, but we'll briefly tiptoe through the fringes of science to make my point.

I once saw a PBS special that talked about the origins of the universe. In this particular episode, experts said that the universe is made up matter, both the kind of matter we can touch, and something called "dark" matter. In fact, experts on the show said our universe may be made up of 95% dark matter, and of just 5% of the matter that we can see and touch. As of today, we know very little about dark matter. In other words, at most we understand only about 5% of the stuff that makes up our universe. And of that 5%, we only know about what's on Earth and in our own solar system. And of that amount, there is still a lot about what we don't know. This tells me that we understand excruciatingly little about our universe.

In order to try to better understand dark matter, scientists have built something in the ground below France and Switzerland called the Large Hadron Collider (LHC). I'm not joking, this is absolutely true. It's not science fiction. Operated by CERN, the European Organization for Nuclear Research, the LHC is a seventeen-mile (twenty-seven kilometer) long underground tunnel in the shape of a circle.[19] The LHC is a particle collider—it sends particles, such as protons, around the circle in opposite directions with the intent to have them collide when they meet. The theory behind creating these collisions is that these collisions could show evidence that dark matter exists, even if we don't actually get to see dark matter. Through this process, scientists have discovered the existence of a particle called "Higgs boson," or as some call it, the "God particle."[20] This discovery won the Nobel Prize in Physics in 2013. This "God particle" apparently plays an essential role in holding matter, and ultimately, the universe together, and is said to be highly related to dark matter. Some say that by understanding the "God particle" and dark matter, we can better understand how the universe was created.

To be sure, this is stuff on the leading edges of science, and I don't understand it very well. But, the whole point of sharing this is to highlight the fact that we know very little about our universe. Interestingly, it's the "stuff" we can't see that may be the most important. Because we know so little about the universe and what we can't see, it limits our ability to make predictions and to understand how everything fits together.

Let's now relate this to media and communication research. Much of the communication research today is conducted under the assumption that the "mind" and the brain are the same thing. When we say we "have something in mind," we're not talking about having a piece of foreign material stuck in our brains. We're talking about the content of our thoughts. Communication researchers, however, see the human brain as simply an organ that is housed in the body, and that when the body dies, so does the mind.

This approach suggests that emotions and thoughts are simply a result of the electrical, chemical, or other biological processes of the brain.[21] This approach also assumes that when the body dies, the human mind ceases to exist because we are simply made up of elements, and that what makes us, *us,* also ceases to exist when we die.

Do you see what I'm pointing out here? All of the research that we've reviewed and that is being conducted today by communication researchers assumes that we are nothing more than a mixture of chemicals and electrical impulses, and that there is no such thing as the mind or the soul. They might be correct. I'm not trying to convince you one way or the other about the existence of the soul. I just want to raise the possibility that something unseen, such as the soul, *could* exist. In fact, research shows that many people and cultures around the world believe that the soul continues to live even after the body dies.[22] Many people believe that our mind, or our soul, is separate from our brain. Many live their lives based on this assumption. In fact, it is because of the complexity and fantastic nature of the brain that psychologists suggest the concept of the soul is so pervasive among many cultures around the world. Some research even suggests that children are born with the concept of the soul, that they are dual beings made up of a soul and a body.[23] Whether you believe in the concept of a soul or not is not the point. The point is that many people live their lives operating under the assumption that they have a soul—an assumption that is not allowed by communication research.

Here's why this matters. If we assume that humans do not have a mind or soul that is separate from the brain, then our reaction to everything we see in the media is simply a biological reaction. In other words, everything we know about children's responses to media exposure is simply their biological response to what they see. And the decisions kids make about media use are simply biologically driven. Their motivation to view programming, play a game, or communicate via their phones is simply biological. Said differently, because media researchers don't allow for the possibility of a soul, the only part of the human experience that we even partially understand is the biological part. Is it possible that we are missing out on a large part of the human experience because we are not allowing for the possibility that humans have souls? Is it possible that the soul is like dark matter—we can't see it, but it may be vital to our understanding of how media affects us? We have little physical evidence that something such as a soul exists. But I suppose it's possible that some, if not many parts of the human experience, relate to how the soul interacts with our environments, including media messages. It's possible, then, that media messages affect our soul, and not just our biology. And even if some people don't believe in the existence of a soul, does the fact that someone does have this belief influence how they see the world?

I recently asked a researcher colleague, someone much smarter than me who studies the brain and how media messages impact the brain, to tell me what the single, most-important motivating influence in their life was. They didn't tell me anything about their brain. They told me about their beliefs and their relationship with their concept of a higher being. I found that very interesting. It seems that even among researchers who work under the assumption that there is no soul, some still believe that the status of their soul may be the most important factor in determining how we view the world. Could it be, then, that media content not only affects our brains, but our souls too? Could it be that media messages have the power to change who we, and our kids, are because the messages can impact our "soul?" Could it be that when we talk about *becoming* a better person, or when we worry about the type of people our children are *becoming*, we're really talking about their mind or their soul? Is it possible that the essence of who an individual is may actually be encapsulated in their mind or their soul, not the chemical reactions of their brains? Could it be that our soul, in cooperation with our brain, helps us make decisions about what to do with media content to which we are exposed?

Again, I'm not trying to convince you one way or another as to the reality of the existence of a soul, but I am saying that because many humans on this planet operate under the implicit assumption that they have a soul, communication researchers need to begin to take "soul" variables into account. Could it be that it's the soul, and not the brain, that controls our emotions, thoughts, and behavioral responses to media exposure? Could it be that we can train the soul, just as we can train the brain, to see the world a certain way? And what would that mean for both our study of media effects and of how we engage in media parenting? Would we look at our kids differently if we could somehow show that their minds/souls (if they have them) are susceptible to media effects? Perhaps we haven't tackled these questions yet because we don't yet know of a way to measure the soul's response to media exposure. Or maybe we're just too afraid to admit that there are some things that our brains just can't understand for now.

What we're talking about is just crazy enough, at least in the academic world, that this is the first time I've discussed these ideas publicly. These are things that just aren't talked about among many academics. But I think it may be time to revisit the fundamental assumptions of how we study children's interactions with media. Allowing for the existence of a soul may help us to better predict how kids are affected by media, why kids choose certain media, and the long-term ramifications of *becoming* in a media-saturated world.

## Seeing Our Kids for Who They Really Are

I believe that one way to motivate parents to be great, powerful media parents is to give them a glimpse of who their children really are. We've discussed a little about what science (or the fringes of science) suggests about who our kids really are and what they're made of. When we consider who our kids can become, whether or not we are talking about their brain or their mind/soul, I hope we can see that who our children become is of utmost importance, and that the goal of media parenting is to help kids reach their potential, to become what their potential suggests they can become. In addition to this detour into a discussion about God particles and souls, perhaps it may also be helpful to share a personal experience to help illustrate what I've learned about who my kids are, the difficulties they work under, and who they can become. The story I'm about to share is personal and true, and it might change the way you see your kids, and how you parent—both in terms of media parenting and otherwise.

Off the coast of Washington State is one of my favorite places in the world—the San Juan Islands, a group of islands in the Pacific Ocean accessible only by ferry or airplane. One summer several years ago, I volunteered with a Boy Scout troop near Portland, Oregon, and we took a group of Boy Scouts to the San Juan Islands for a weeklong bike trip.

We parked all of our transport cars in the city of Anacortes, on the mainland of Washington State. We boarded the ferry with just our bikes and one supply truck driven by a former Marine named Bill (names in this story have been changed to protect privacy). Our first stop was Lopez Island, a quiet island covered with lavender farms and towering Douglas fir trees. As we departed the ferry that first day and began our short bike ride to the state park where we would camp for the night, it quickly became apparent that one of the boys, Robert, was struggling to keep up with everyone else. He soon fell far behind, and trailed into camp last—just in front of the supply truck. In my mind, I silently resented Robert for being lazy and for not keeping up with the group.

This pattern continued for the next several days. We would bike to the next viewpoint to watch whales or explore a lighthouse, and Robert would pedal in well after everyone else, trailed slowly by Bill and the supply truck. Robert was the one kid on the trip that came because his mother told him he had to, and I began to wish he had just stayed home.

Near the end of the trip, we took a ferry to Orcas Island, a beautiful island shaped like a horseshoe, kind of like my other favorite place in the world—Ohio Stadium. The main feature of Orcas Island is Mt. Constitution, one of the most prominent features of the San Juan Islands. On top of Mt. Constitution is a tower from which you can see all the way from British Columbia to the north to Mt. Rainier on the other side of Seattle to the south. The road to the top of Mt. Constitution is only about five miles long, but it rises roughly 2,500 feet in those brief five miles. We came up with what we thought was a brilliant challenge. We wanted to see if we could get to the top of the mountain without letting our feet touch the ground, without stopping on our bikes. So, early in the morning, we all lined our bikes up at the base of the mountain and waited for the signal to start. Bill would be driving up and down the hill picking up stragglers. As for Robert, I'm not sure he even started up the hill. I think he just climbed into the supply truck with Bill, because I soon saw Bill taking Robert to the top of the mountain where they would wait for us. As they drove past, I saw a huge grin on Robert's face that seemed to scream "sucker" to me, and as they disappeared around the next switchback, I resented Robert for being so weak-willed and undetermined.

One by one, boys tired out and stopped, and soon enough Bill would come back down the mountain, pick them up, and drive them to the top, as if there was no shame in someone not reaching the top without stopping. Those of us who made it to the top, however, didn't make it alone. As Bill drove past, he offered words of encouragement, and seeing him drive up and down the hill that day gave us hope that if we stumbled, someone would be there to pick us up.

The next day, we rode to San Juan Island, the most populated of the islands in the group. As we rode to our campground for the night, I once again noticed Robert lagging behind. Fed up with his laziness, I decided to stop and wait for him. When he caught up to me, he complained that no matter how hard he tried, his bike just couldn't keep up with everyone. He was frustrated, and so was I. Wanting to prove to him that the cause of his slowness was him, and not the bike, I traded bikes with him. No less than thirty seconds later, Robert had caught up with the rest of the group, and I fell further and further behind. I rolled into camp that night last. Even the supply truck made it there before me. I had discovered what Robert knew all along, and it took riding his bike to learn several valuable lessons. First, Robert's bike was a piece of junk.

But more importantly, I learned that in life, we have all been given different bikes to ride. This applies especially to our children. Some kids ride the bike of physical or mental disability. Some kids ride the bike of a lack of self-confidence, of families plagued by under-employment, of loneliness, bullying, hurt, abuse, sickness, going to a new school for the first time, trouble with other kids at school, and pain in all its various forms. Some kids are athletic, some aren't. Some are musically inclined, while others are tone deaf. Kids are all given different bikes to ride. And some of those bikes have square tires.

Through this experience, I also learned that no matter what bike our children are asked to ride in life, they will all fail to make it to the top of the mountain by themselves. Call the mountain what you will—completing the fourth grade, overcoming a learning disability, making friends, standing up to a bully—none of our children, not even the strongest and brightest, can make it to that destination without the help of a Bill, of someone willing to descend from the top of the mountain to pick them up and help them. Every one of our kids needs a champion, no matter the bike they are asked to ride up the hill. Every child needs someone to give encouragement, someone to help bear their heavy loads. As parents, we have the responsibility and ability to push them, pull them, and carry them up the hill. We've been up many of the hills that our children will have to climb, and they need us to share what we've learned.

Perhaps equally important, riding Robert's bike that day allowed me to see him for who he really was. He was just a kid struggling with a poorly engineered bike. And seeing him through this lens—through the lens of empathy—has done a few things for me. If I could go back to that trip, I would ask Robert if he would trade bikes for the entire bike trip. It hurts me to know how much he struggled and how those struggles made him feel about himself. I want to see the smile on his face again after he realized that he wasn't weak, that he wasn't a misfit, that the problem wasn't with him, when he saw himself for who he really was. Seeing him this way sparked a motivation in me to serve him. And that's really the crux of this discussion. When we see our children for who they really are— as little people struggling to find their way in life—we want to be more compassionate, spend more time with them, get down on the floor and let them choose the activity. Parenting, including media parenting, becomes a whole lot easier, and infinitely more enjoyable, when we step back and see children for who they really are. When we see them for who they really are, and who they can become, we'll turn off the TV a bit more. We'll go outside and shoot baskets with them. We'll sit down and read them a book. Even when we don't want to.

A few years ago, I went on another camping trip, this time with my family. We had pitched our tents and were sitting around the campfire getting ready for bed. It must have been nearly eleven p.m. when we saw an SUV pull up, carrying one of our friends and about nine kids, some hers, some not. This friend had to drive nearly three hours to get there that night, and I asked her why she even bothered. She responded with an insightful question, "Why should I deprive the kids of these opportunities just because I don't want to do it?"

Seeing kids for who they really are changes us. It changes everything.

## The Media Maze

They may not know it consciously, but our kids are trying to figure their way through the media maze. Their brains, and maybe their souls, are still developing. And they need all the help they can get to make sense of the world.

Like you, I feel very inadequate when it comes to raising my kids. This is, after all, my first time being a parent. I know I've made some mistakes, and I know I'll make even more. And like you, I hope that my kids can make it in life despite the things I do that have the potential to screw them up. But I feel hopeful for the future. I think we all have great reason to hope. I'll illustrate why, and finish *Media Maze* in the same way we started, with a story about one of my daughters.

Somebody once said that a singing child is a happy child. If that's true, then one of my daughters is the happiest kid in the world, because she seems to always be singing. At the dinner table. In the car. Doing homework. Always. She feels happiness very strongly. She also feels other emotions very strongly. We've told her that it's always okay to feel emotions, but we've had many talks about what we do with those emotions and about how to control them. During one especially tough day, when she was feeling and expressing lots of emotions, I asked her why she felt it was okay to express these emotions in such a dramatic way at home but not at other places. Her answered surprised me, and this is what gives me hope. She said, "Because I feel safe at home."

So, when I think that I'm not doing enough as a parent, when I feel like I just mess things up when I do try, when I wonder if I'm giving enough, I remember that my daughter feels safe at home. Safe to share. Safe to vent and listen. Safe to be herself and try new things. Safe to become.

The media maze is scary. There are things seemingly lurking around every corner. There are dead ends that we don't know about until we bump into them. If through our media parenting we can help our kids feel safe and free to be themselves, is there really anything more we can ask of ourselves?

I suppose, then, that my wife and I are doing something right as parents. And so are you, even if you don't think you are. My hope is that *Media Maze* has sparked some ideas, has given you some confidence, and has increased your desire to be a media parent intent on being more than a default parent.

Parenting is tough. Media parenting is an increasingly large part of that difficult task. But it's worth our every effort to empower our kids with the tools they need to navigate the media maze.

## Notes

1. Albert Hastorf and Hadley Cantril, "They Saw a Game; A Case Study," *The Journal of Abnormal and Social Psychology* 49, no. 1 (1954): 129-134, doi: 10.1037/h0057880.
2. Ibid, 129.
3. Ibid, 132.
4. Ronak Pate, R. Nathan Spreng, and Gary Turner, "Functional Brain Changes Following Cognitive and Motor Skills Training: A Quantitative Meta-Analysis," *Neurorehabilitation and Neural Repair* 27, no. 3 (2013): 187-199, doi: 10.1177/1545968312461718.
5. Karene Booker, "Scientists Discover How Brains Change with New Skills," *Cornell Chronicle,* April 4, 2013, http://news.cornell.edu/stories/2013/04/scientists-discover-how-brains-change-new-skills.
6. Harvard Mental Health Letter, "How Addiction Hijacks the Brain," *Harvard Health Publications, Harvard Medical School,* July 2011, www.health.harvard.edu/newsletter_article/how-addiction-hijacks-the-brain.
7. Nick Lee, Amanda Broderick and Laura Chamberlain, "What is 'Neuromarketing'? A Discussion and Agenda for Future Research," *International Journal of Psychophysiology* 63, no. 2 (2007): 199-204, doi: 10.1016.j.ijpsycho.2006.03.007.
8. Vaughan Bell, "The Marketing Industry Has Started Using Neuroscience, But the Results are More Glitter Than Gold," *The Guardian,* June 28, 2015, www.theguardian.com/science/2015/jun/28/vaughan-bell-neuroscience-marketing-advertising.
9. Brian Knutson et al., "Neural Predictors of Purchases," *Neuron* 53, no. 1 (2007): 147-156, doi: 10.1016/j.neuron.2006.11.010.
10. Simone Kühn, Enrique Strelow, and Jürgen Gallinat, "Multiple 'Buy Buttons' in the Brain: Forecasting Chocolate Sales at Point-of-Sale Based on Functional Brain Activation Using fMRI," *NeuroImage* 136, no. 1 (2016): 122-128, doi: 10.1016/j.neuroimage.2016.05.021.

11. Russ Fazio, "On the Automatic Activation of Associated Evaluations: An Overview," *Cognition and Emotion* 15, no. 2 (2001): 115-141, doi: 10.1080/02699930125908.

12. Carl Fulwiler et al., "Keeping Weight Off: Study Protocol of an RCT to Investigate Brain Changes Associated with Mindfulness-Based Stress Reduction," *BMJ Open* 6, no. 11 (2016): doi: 10.1136/bmjopen-2016-012573.

13. Mindful, "The Body Scan Practice," *Mindful,* November 7, 2012, https://www.mindful.org/the-body-scan-practice/.

14. Rinske Gotink et al., "8-Week Mindfulness Based Stress Reduction Induces Brain Changes Similar to Traditional Long-Term Meditation Practice: A Systematic Review," *Brain and Cognition* 108, (2016): 32-41, doi: 10.1016/j.bandc.2016.07.001.

15. Including the prefrontal cortex, hippocampus, insula, and cingulate cortex regions of participants' brains.

16. Robin Nabi, "Emotion and Media Effects," in *The Sage Handbook of Media Processes and Effects,* eds. Robin Nabi and Mary Beth Oliver (Thousand Oaks, CA: SAGE, 2009), 205-221.

17. Douglas Gentile, Edward Swing, Craig Anderson, Daniel Rinker, and Kathleen Thomas, "Differential Neural Recruitment During Violent Video Game Play in Violent—and Nonviolent—Game Players," *Psychology of Popular Media Culture* 5, no. 1 (2016): 39-51, doi: 10.1037/ppm0000009.

18. Ibid, 48.

19. "About CERN," *CERN,* accessed June 22, 2017, https://home.cern/about.

20. Editors of Scientific American, *The Higgs Boson: Searching for the God Particle* (New York: Scientific American, eBook, 2017).

21. Annie Lang, Robert Potter, and Paul Bolls, "Where Psychophysiology Meets the Media: Taking the Effects Out of Mass Media Research," in *Media Effects: Advances in Theory and Research*, 3rd ed., eds. Jennings Bryant and Mary Beth Oliver (New York: Routledge, 2009), 185-206.

22. For a review, see Rebekah Richert and Paul Harris, "Dualism Revisited: Body vs. Mind vs. Soul," *Journal of Cognition and Culture* 8 (2008): 99-115, doi: 10.1163/156770908X280224.

23. For a review, see Rebekah Richert and Paul Harris, "The Ghost in My Body: Children's Developing Concept of the Soul," *Journal of Cognition and Culture* 6, no. 3-4 (2006): 409-428, doi: 10.1163/156853706778554913.

# Appendix

As you noticed in the preceding chapters, I referred quite a bit to the media's portrayal of women. Well, surprise, there is more about the topic that I feel its important we discuss that I just couldn't seem to fit in elsewhere. So the few paragraphs that make up this Appendix will suffice.

## Media Portrayals of Women's Intelligence

Because women on TV are so often portrayed as sex objects, they are often not portrayed in ways that show them to be intelligent. Because of this, many believe that women aren't cut out for jobs that require the use of their brain, such as jobs in science or technology. You may have seen the 2017 study[1] showing that young girls think boys are smarter than girls. Media, other research shows, plays a strong role in how girls view themselves. To understand where the stereotype that women aren't cut out for "scientific" jobs comes from, we must first look at a classic 1957 study.[2] The study asked more than 30,000 US high school students to describe what image comes to mind when they think of a scientist—the picture they most often described was that of a middle-age man in a white lab coat and glasses. The study, or iterations of it, has been corroborated many times in the ensuing years among hundreds of thousands of people in dozens of countries. And these stereotypes seem to begin as early as elementary school. When they are asked to draw a scientist, elementary school kids' pictures most often portray a male scientist.

Now, I'm not necessarily concerned that young girls think most scientists are male, because that perception is actually correct. More men fill "scientific" and "technology" career roles than women, for what I'm sure are a variety of reasons. But, what I'm most concerned about is the fact that girls don't even consider careers in science because they don't think they're smart enough. Perhaps that's where the problem lies. Decades of research show that if you think you can do something, you're more likely to try it out—it's called self-efficacy, and self-efficacy is one of the strongest predictors of future behavior. If girls don't believe they can do something, they're less likely to even try.

For some reason, girls don't think they're as smart as boys. To change this, research suggests, we need to change girls' self-efficacy—their belief that they have the ability to accomplish *something*. But, I think even that wouldn't be enough. I want my daughters to believe that they can accomplish *anything*. If we were to boil down all the media effects research into one statement it might be this: whatever we fill our minds with, that's what we become. Think about it. If children watch violence, research shows they can become aggressive. If kids watch sex on TV, they are more likely to engage in risky sexual behaviors. If girls see women on TV portrayed as meant only for fulfilling a man's desire, what are they supposed to think? If women in the media are portrayed as less intelligent than men, of course girls will pick up on that.

So, to me it makes perfect sense that if we want girls to feel good about themselves, and to feel like they can accomplish anything, we need to fill their minds with that message. And that message needs to be louder than the messages they get about girls from the media. Because the message about their potential and their worth is so rarely found in media, I believe it is up to parents to take a leading role in changing how girls think about themselves. If media tells girls that men are smarter, parents need to tell them how smart girls are ten times as much. If media tells girls that their value lies in their appearance, we must tell them time and time again that their value is (1) intrinsic and (2) based on who they are, not on what they look like.

Let me tell you how we're trying to do this in our family. When *Hidden Figures* came out in the theater, we took all four of our daughters to see it. If you haven't seen it, please do. In short, the movie shares the story of three black women mathematicians who become some of the most important behind-the-scenes figures in the 1960s space race. Afterward, we talked with our girls about the show and emphasized as strongly as we could that because of strong women of the past, they can become whoever and whatever they want. I look forward to the day when being a strong, brilliant woman is something so commonplace that a movie telling the story isn't even necessary to get girls to consider that they can do anything. Our work with our daughters, of course, is not done. We'll need to tell them this same message week after week, month after month, year after year. And your daughters (and sons) need you to do the same.

I don't pretend to be an expert on women's issues—women's rights, women's gender roles, what it means to be a woman, etc.—but I do know that nobody has a greater influence on children than parents. And it's time for us to take our girls back from the media by reenthroning media parenting as *the* best solution for helping our daughters believe in themselves.

## Boys, Girls, and Sexting

Research suggests that adolescent boys hold girls to some striking double standards when it comes to sexting. One study involving fifty-one adolescents, a mix of both girls and boys in three different American cities, asked participants to respond to several open-ended questions about sexting.[3] Researchers analyzed their responses and found that boys judge girls' sexting behaviors in one of two ways. First, boys think that girls who send sexts are "crazy, insecure, attention-seeking sluts with poor judgment." At the same time, however, boys categorized girls who didn't send sexts as "prude," "goody," or "stuck up." So, what's a girl to do? Send a sext and be considered a whore, or not send a sext and be thought of as a snob? As parents, the answer is clear, but it's not so clear to girls. Girls in the study said they feel that if they don't send sexts to boys, then they'd lose their chance to have a desirable relationship with a boy. One girl in the study said this about the pressure she felt to send sexts to her boyfriend: "I felt like if I didn't do it, they wouldn't continue to talk to me." And another girl said that "if we don't send them they will think we aren't outgoing and get mad." In other words, in their search for approval and acceptance, girls feel serious social pressure to send risqué photos to boys.

Ugh, so now what? This is where I once again leave research behind and share my own educated, albeit biased, opinion. First, as I've already mentioned, I think the responsibility to teach kids about media, including sexting, falls on parents, not on schools or other forms of government. A school's job is to educate, not to dictate right from wrong. I am highly against government censorship—yes, even of pornography—because allowing the government to dictate what's right and wrong can lead to, well, most of the problems that we see in government policy today. That means we take the good with the bad. It also means that it's not enough to teach kids about the potential legal implications of sexting—it can be considered, by the way, a form of child pornography punishable by law (I think schools can and should tell this to kids). No, the explanation for rules about sexting shouldn't just be that much of it might be against the law. This is treating symptoms, not the cause. I think the fight against sexting has to be conducted on a much deeper level, and that means parents have to share their opinions about the effects of sexting. And when it comes to sexting, those effects can hit at a level as deep as a child's core self-worth.

Thankfully, we haven't had to deal with sexting specifically in our family. Fingers crossed. We have, however, tried to be preemptive about issues like this—we don't do it perfectly, but we're at least trying. In our house this takes the form of talking with our kids about what makes them valuable and special. We try to teach our kids that their worth is not, and never will be, based on their body or their appearance. Sure, we want our kids to practice good hygiene and to work hard to be strong and healthy. But we also try to teach them that it doesn't matter what other people think of them. It matters more what they think of themselves. Kids—both boys and girls—need to be taught that it's never okay to objectify or to be objectified—and that's exactly what sexting does to girls. It objectifies them. It turns them into commodities, as visual representations of cultural ideals. Our daughters are not things. They're not images to be exploited for a boy's jollies. I hold to the pie-in-the-sky ideal that when boys and girls understand this, boys will no longer pressure a girl to send a sext, and girls will be empowered to overcome any pressure to send a sext.

## Notes

1.  Lin Bian, Sarah-Jane Leslie, and Andrei Cimpian, "Gender Stereotypes About Intellectual Ability Emerge Early and Influence Children's Interests," *Science* 355, no 6323 (2017): 389-391, doi: 10.1126/science.aah6524.

2.  Margaret Mead and Rhoda Métraux, "Image of the Scientist Among High-School Students," *Science* 126, no. 3270 (1957): 384-390, doi: 10.1126/science.126.3270.384.

3.  Julia Lippman and Scott Campbell, "Damned If You Do, Damned If You Don't . . . If You're a Girl: Relational and Normative Contexts of Adolescent Sexting in the United States," *Journal of Children and Media* 8, no. 4 (2014): 371-386, doi: 10.1080/17482798.2014.923009.

# Acknowledgments

Chasten, who never laughs out loud at my crazy projects, ideas, and philosophizing; who believes that reality includes big dreams; who hangs around even when I'm not hang-around-able; and who will always be my superior.

My daughters, who always laugh at my dad jokes, who think I'm much cooler than I really am, and who are fulfilling my greatest desire by turning out just like their mom.

Debbie Angelos, Nollie Haws, and Rebecca Lucero, for their constructive feedback and support.

Cedar Fort and my editors, who took a chance on me.

All the children and media scholars, whose research is changing the world one study, one family, and one child at a time.

# About the Author

ERIC RASMUSSEN, PhD, is a children and media researcher, college professor, and the author of ChildrenAndMediaMan.com. He has published numerous articles in peer-reviewed academic journals related to media parenting and the effects of media on children. He received a doctorate in communication from The Ohio State University. He now lives in Lubbock, Texas, with his wife and children.

SCAN TO VISIT

CHILDRENANDMEDIAMAN.COM